D0617949

Southern Living
Everyday
MENUS

Oxmoor House

Southern Living Everyday MENUS

SOUTHERN LIVING
EDITOR: Shannon Sliter Satterwhite
ART DIRECTOR: Claudia Hon
COPY CHIEF: Julia Pittard Coker
COPY EDITOR: Cindy Riegle
PRODUCTION COORDINATOR: Christy Coleman

FOODS EDITOR: Scott Jones
SENIOR WRITER: Donna Florio
ASSOCIATE FOODS EDITORS: Charla Draper, Shirley Harrington, Holley Johnson, Kate Nicholson, Mary Allen Perry
ASSISTANT FOODS EDITOR: Vicki A. Poellnitz   ASSISTANT RECIPE EDITOR: John McMillan
TEST KITCHENS DIRECTOR: Lyda H. Jones   ASSISTANT TEST KITCHENS DIRECTOR: James Schend
TEST KITCHENS SPECIALIST/FOOD STYLING: Vanessa A. McNeil
TEST KITCHENS PROFESSIONALS: Marian Cairns, Rebecca Kracke Gordon, Pam Lolley, Alyssa Porubcan, Angela Sellers

SENIOR PHOTOGRAPHERS: Ralph Anderson, Van Chaplin, Joseph De Sciose, Art Meripol, John O'Hagan, Allen Rokach, Mark Sandlin, Charles Walton IV
PHOTOGRAPHERS: Jim Bathie, Gary Clark, Tina Cornett, William Dickey, Beth Dreiling, Laurey W. Glenn, Meg McKinney
ASSISTANT PHOTOGRAPHER: Mary Margaret Chambliss
SENIOR PHOTO STYLIST: Buffy Hargett   ASSOCIATE PHOTO STYLIST: Alan Henderson
PHOTO STYLIST: Rose Nguyen   ASSISTANT PHOTO STYLISTS: Lisa Powell Bailey, Cari South
PHOTO SERVICES DIRECTOR: Anne Nathews Griffin
PHOTO LIBRARIAN: Tracy Duncan   PHOTO PRODUCTION MANAGER: Larry Hunter
PHOTO SERVICES: Amanda Leigh Abbett, Ginny P. Allen, Catherine Carr, Lisa Dawn Love

EDITOR IN CHIEF: John Alex Floyd, Jr.
MANAGING EDITOR: Clay Nordan
EXECUTIVE EDITORS: Derick Belden, Susan Dosier, Warner McGowin, Dianne Young
DEPUTY EDITOR: Kenner Patton
ART DIRECTOR: Craig Smith
COPY CHIEF: Dawn P. Cannon
PRODUCTION AND COLOR QUALITY MANAGER: Katie Terrell Morrow
CREATIVE DEVELOPMENT DIRECTOR: Valerie Fraser Luesse
PHOTOGRAPHY AND COVER ART DIRECTOR: Jon Thompson
ASSISTANT TO THE EDITOR IN CHIEF: Marian Cooper
OFFICE MANAGER: Wanda T. Stephens
ADMINISTRATIVE ASSISTANTS: Chris Carrier Garmon, Lynne Long, Sandra J. Thomas
EDITORIAL ASSISTANTS: Karen Brechin, Catherine K. Russell
ASSISTANT ART DIRECTOR: Gae Watson
SENIOR DESIGNERS: Patricia See Hooten, Jennie McClain Shannon
DESIGNER: Amy Kathryn R. Merk
DESIGNER/ILLUSTRATOR: Christopher Davis
ASSISTANT COPY CHIEF: Paula Hughes
COPY EDITOR: Rhonda Richards
ASSISTANT COPY EDITORS: Jacqueline M. Fogas, Libby Monteith Minor, JoAnn Weatherly
COPY ASSISTANTS: Katie Bowlby, Leah Dueffer, Stephanie Gibson Mims
ASSISTANT PRODUCTION MANAGER: Jamie Barnhart
PRODUCTION ASSISTANT: Allison Brooke Krannich
ONLINE EDITOR: Robin Anne Spooner
ASSOCIATE ONLINE EDITOR: Carlton Riley Smith
EDITORIAL CONTRIBUTORS: Ashley Arthur, Tara Ivey

OXMOOR HOUSE, INC.
EDITOR IN CHIEF: Nancy Fitzpatrick Wyatt
EXECUTIVE EDITOR: Susan Carlisle Payne
ART DIRECTOR: Cynthia Rose Cooper
COPY CHIEF: Allison Long Lowery
EDITOR: McCharen Pratt
DESIGNER: Emily Albright Parrish
COPY EDITOR: Diane Rose
EDITORIAL ASSISTANT: Brigette Gaucher
EDITORIAL INTERN: Mary Catherine Shamblin

SOUTHERN LIVING AT HOME®
VICE PRESIDENT & EXECUTIVE DIRECTOR: Dianne Mooney
DIRECTOR OF DESIGN: Melanie Grant

Southern Living Everyday Menus
©2005 by Oxmoor House, Inc.
Book Division of Southern Progress Corporation
P.O. Box 2262, Birmingham, Alabama 35201-2262

ISBN: 0-8487-3130-1
Printed in the United States of America
First Printing 2005

All rights reserved. No part of this book may be reproduced in any form or by any means without the prior written permission of the publisher, excepting brief quotations in connection with reviews written specifically for inclusion in magazines or newspapers, or limited excerpts strictly for personal use.

Some products in this book are from current and previous *Southern Living At HOME®* catalogs. Current products are available for purchase.

Southern Living is a registered trademark of Southern Living, Inc., U.S. Patent and Trademark Office.

Created exclusively for *Southern Living At HOME®*, the Direct Selling Company of Southern Progress Corporation. For more information about *Southern Living At HOME®*, please write to: Consultant Services, P.O. Box 830951, Birmingham, AL 35283-0951.

contents

cover photography: Tina Cornett;
styling: Buffy Hargett; food styling: Pam Lolley

Dear Friends,

Whether you're a beginner in the kitchen or a seasoned cook, busy lives require simple solutions. Let *Southern Living At HOME*® come to the rescue with this easy-to-follow menu guide that offers a nice change of pace—easy weeknight recipes, quick serving suggestions, and time-saving ways to plan ahead. We even tell you how long you will spend in the kitchen with our new hands-on, hands-off approach. "Hands on" includes how much time you'll spend measuring, chopping, or sautéing; "hands off" estimates the walk-away time you'll have while a recipe bakes, chills, freezes, and even simmers (with occasional stirring).

Get a head start with our "Ready When You Are" chapter that begins on page 24, featuring some of our favorite make-ahead meals and recipes using last night's leftovers. Plus, we'll tell you about a convenient, versatile ingredient that has made my weeknights more manageable—rotisserie chicken from the supermarket deli. For party-planning basics, flip to "Casual Entertaining" on page 84, and learn some stress-free strategies for your next gathering.

Each doable section offers something for everyone, and I hope these menu ideas make every day a little easier for you.

Shannon

Shannon Sliter Satterwhite
Editor

Meatloaf and Mashed Potatoes

Have a comforting plate of Herbed Meatloaf With Tomato Gravy, crisp-tender asparagus, and your favorite mashed potatoes.

Meatloaf is quite possibly the perfect use of ground beef. Just combine it with eggs, breadcrumbs, and a few flavorful ingredients for an easy main dish. Pair it with mashed potatoes and a favorite vegetable, and you've got a simple meal the whole family will love. Save the leftovers for meatloaf sandwiches the next day, or freeze individual servings for a meal on the go.

REUBEN LOAF

Makes 8 servings
Hands on: 20 min., Hands off: 50 min.

2 (12-ounce) cans corned beef, crumbled
2 cups soft breadcrumbs
2 large eggs
2 tablespoons chopped fresh parsley
1/4 teaspoon garlic salt
1 (14-ounce) can chopped sauerkraut, drained
1 cup (4 ounces) shredded Swiss cheese
1/2 teaspoon caraway seeds
3 (1-ounce) Swiss cheese slices, cut in half diagonally

STIR together crumbled corned beef, breadcrumbs, and next 3 ingredients in a bowl; shape into a 10-inch square on a sheet of heavy-duty plastic wrap. Wipe bowl clean.

PRESS sauerkraut between paper towels to remove excess moisture. Combine sauerkraut, shredded Swiss cheese, and caraway seeds in bowl; spoon down center of meat mixture.

FOLD sides of meat mixture over sauerkraut mixture, lifting plastic wrap as needed. Remove plastic wrap. Press edges and ends of meat mixture to seal, and place, seam side down, in a lightly greased 13- x 9-inch pan.

BAKE at 350° for 45 minutes or until beef is no longer pink in center. Arrange cheese slices on top, and bake 5 more minutes. Serve immediately.

HERBED MEATLOAF WITH TOMATO GRAVY

Makes 6 servings
Hands on: 30 min., Hands off: 55 min.

1 (8-ounce) jar dried tomatoes in oil
1 medium onion, diced
1 green bell pepper, diced
2 garlic cloves, pressed
1 3/4 pounds ground round
2 large eggs
1 whole wheat bread slice, torn into small pieces
1/2 cup (2 ounces) shredded sharp provolone cheese
2 teaspoons dried basil
1 teaspoon dried oregano
1 teaspoon pepper
1/2 teaspoon salt
1/2 teaspoon dried thyme
Tomato Gravy

DRAIN dried tomatoes, reserving 1 tablespoon oil. Reserve 6 tomatoes for Tomato Gravy. Chop remaining tomatoes.

HEAT reserved 1 tablespoon tomato oil in a large skillet over medium-high heat; add onion, bell pepper, and garlic. Sauté 5 minutes or until tender. Stir in chopped tomatoes, ground round, and next 8 ingredients. Shape into a loaf, and place in a lightly greased 9- x 5-inch loafpan.

BAKE at 350° for 55 minutes or until beef is no longer pink in center. Remove from pan, reserving 1/4 cup drippings for Tomato Gravy. Keep meatloaf warm, and serve with gravy.

Tomato Gravy:
Hands on: 20 min.

1 1/4 cups milk
2 1/2 tablespoons all-purpose flour
6 reserved dried tomatoes, chopped
1/4 cup reserved meatloaf drippings
1 tablespoon diced green onions
1/4 teaspoon salt
1/4 teaspoon dried basil
1/8 teaspoon pepper

WHISK together 1 1/4 cups milk and flour in a saucepan until smooth. Whisk in remaining ingredients. Cook mixture over medium heat, whisking constantly, 10 minutes or until thickened.

CREAMY MASHED POTATOES IN AN INSTANT

Makes 4 servings
Hands on: 10 min.

1 cup milk
1 cup water
1 1/2 cups instant mashed potato flakes
1 (8-ounce) container softened cream cheese
3 green onions, chopped
1/4 teaspoon salt
1/4 teaspoon pepper

COMBINE milk and 1 cup water in a microwave-safe bowl; add potato flakes, stirring just until moistened.

MICROWAVE at HIGH 3 to 3 1/2 minutes.

ADD cream cheese, green onions, salt, and pepper, stirring until smooth. Serve immediately.

STIR IN MORE FLAVOR

These bonus recipe variations work for both Creamy Mashed Potatoes In an Instant and From the Freezer (see page 7).

MEXICAN MASHED POTATOES: Substitute 1 cup shredded Monterey Jack cheese with peppers for cream cheese, and omit green onions and pepper.

JAZZY MASHED POTATOES: Substitute 1/2 cup sour cream for cream cheese and 2 tablespoons chopped chives for green onions; stir in 1/4 cup grated Parmesan cheese.

DILL-SOUR CREAM MASHED POTATOES: Substitute 1/3 cup sour cream for cream cheese and 1/2 teaspoon dried dillweed for green onions.

PESTO MASHED POTATOES: Omit cream cheese, green onions, and salt; stir 1/4 cup pesto sauce into hot potatoes.

GARLIC MASHED POTATOES: Omit cream cheese and green onions. Melt 3 tablespoons butter in a skillet; add 4 garlic cloves, pressed. Cook over medium heat, stirring constantly, 1 minute or until garlic is lightly browned. Stir into hot potatoes. ▶

Lean ground beef, fat-free milk, and egg substitute lighten up Individual Meatloaves without sacrificing flavor. Serve with steamed green beans and Smoky Mashed Potato Bake.

INDIVIDUAL MEATLOAVES

Makes 6 servings
Hands on: 20 min.; Hands off: 1 hr., 10 min.

YOU CAN REDUCE SODIUM BY OMITTING SEASONED SALT AND USING ONLY HALF A BOTTLE OF CHILI SAUCE.

2 pounds lean ground beef
1 tablespoon reduced-sodium Worcestershire sauce
½ teaspoon seasoned salt
½ teaspoon seasoned pepper
1 medium onion, minced
5 white bread slices, crusts removed
½ cup fat-free milk
¼ cup egg substitute
1½ cups soft breadcrumbs
1 (12-ounce) bottle chili sauce
½ cup boiling water

COMBINE ground beef and next 4 ingredients; set aside.

CUT bread into small pieces. Place bread, milk, and egg substitute in a large bowl. Beat at medium speed with an electric mixer until blended.

STIR meat mixture into egg mixture. Shape mixture into 6 loaves; roll in 1½ cups soft breadcrumbs.

ARRANGE loaves in a lightly greased 13- x 9-inch pan. Spread chili sauce over loaves. Pour ½ cup boiling water into pan.

BAKE at 350° for 1 hour or until beef is no longer pink in center. Let stand 10 minutes before serving.

SMOKY MASHED POTATO BAKE

Makes 10 servings
Hands on: 30 min., Hands off: 55 min.

3½ pounds new potatoes, cut into 1-inch pieces
3 garlic cloves, minced
1 teaspoon olive oil
Vegetable cooking spray
¾ cup (3 ounces) shredded smoked Gouda cheese
1 cup fat-free half-and-half
2 to 3 chipotle peppers in adobo sauce, minced
½ cup light margarine
½ (8-ounce) package fat-free cream cheese, softened
½ teaspoon salt

COOK potatoes in a large Dutch oven in boiling water to cover 30 minutes or

successful loafing

- It might feel strange, but your hands make the best mixer. Don't be afraid to use them to knead ingredients into the meat.
- An instant-read thermometer, which quickly registers the temperature of the center of the meatloaf, is a fail-safe way to check for doneness. Make sure the thermometer reaches at least 160°. Sometimes the meatloaf pulls away from the sides of the pan before it is fully cooked.
- Let meatloaf stand at room temperature 10 minutes before cutting so that the slices will hold their shape better.
- To prevent the fat drippings from accumulating in the bottom of the pan, use a nonstick meatloaf pan with an insert. The insert has holes on the bottom, allowing fat to drain from the meatloaf into a reservoir. Look for one at your local discount store, or visit www.target.com.

For deliciously creamy mashed potatoes without the fuss, use our frozen or instant variations.

until tender; drain and set aside.

SAUTÉ garlic in hot oil in a small skillet coated with cooking spray over medium-high heat 2 to 3 minutes or until tender.

MASH potatoes in a large bowl. Stir in garlic, ¼ cup Gouda cheese, half-and-half, and next 4 ingredients until blended. Spoon mixture into a 13- x 9-inch baking dish coated with cooking spray. Sprinkle evenly with remaining ½ cup Gouda.

BAKE at 350° for 30 minutes or until cheese melts.

BARBECUED MEATLOAF

Makes 6 servings
Hands on: 20 min.; Hands off: 1 hr., 10 min.

1½ pounds ground beef
1 cup soft breadcrumbs
1 small onion, chopped
1 large egg
1 teaspoon salt
¼ teaspoon pepper
1 (16-ounce) can tomato sauce, divided
3 tablespoons brown sugar
3 tablespoons white vinegar
2 tablespoons prepared mustard
2 teaspoons Worcestershire sauce

COMBINE first 6 ingredients; stir in ½ cup tomato sauce. Shape into an 8- x 4-inch loaf. Place on a lightly greased rack in a broiler pan. Set aside.

COMBINE remaining tomato sauce, brown sugar, and next 3 ingredients in a saucepan. Bring to a boil over medium heat; reduce heat, and simmer, stirring often, 10 minutes.

BAKE meatloaf at 350° for 50 minutes or until beef is no longer pink in center; baste with tomato sauce mixture, and

bake 10 more minutes. Let stand 10 minutes, and serve with remaining sauce.

INDIVIDUAL BARBECUED MEATLOAVES: Shape meat mixture into 6 loaves, and bake at 350° for 15 minutes; baste with tomato sauce mixture, and bake 10 more minutes or until beef is no longer pink in center. To make ahead, place unbaked loaves in an airtight container, and top with remaining sauce; freeze up to 1 month. Thaw in refrigerator overnight, and bake at 350° for 20 minutes. Bake frozen loaves at 350° for 35 minutes. Let stand 10 minutes before serving.

MEXICAN MEATLOAF

Makes 6 servings
Hands on: 10 min.; Hand off: 1 hr., 15 min.

1 (8-ounce) jar taco sauce
1½ pounds ground beef
2 large eggs
2 to 3 jalapeño peppers, seeded and minced
⅓ cup soft breadcrumbs
½ teaspoon salt
¼ cup chopped onion
⅓ cup (1.3 ounces) shredded Monterey Jack cheese

COMBINE ½ cup taco sauce and next 6 ingredients; shape into a 9- x 5-inch loaf. Place on a lightly greased rack in a broiler pan. Top with remaining taco sauce.

BAKE at 325° for 1 hour or until beef is no longer pink in center. Sprinkle with cheese, and bake 5 more minutes. Let stand 10 minutes before serving.

INDIVIDUAL MEXICAN MEATLOAVES: Shape mixture into 6 loaves, and bake at 325° for 30 minutes or until beef is no longer pink in center. To make ahead,

CREAMY MASHED POTATOES FROM THE FREEZER

Makes 4 servings
Hands on: 10 min., Hands off: 5 min.

TO MAKE AHEAD, PREPARE ANY RECIPE VARIATION (SEE PAGE 5), AND PLACE IN A LIGHTLY GREASED 1-QUART BAKING DISH; COVER AND REFRIGERATE OVERNIGHT. REMOVE FROM REFRIGERATOR, AND LET STAND AT ROOM TEMPERATURE 30 MINUTES; BAKE AT 350° FOR 25 MINUTES.

2⅔ cups frozen mashed potatoes
1⅓ cups milk
1 (8-ounce) container softened cream cheese
3 green onions, chopped
½ teaspoon salt
¼ teaspoon pepper

PREPARE potatoes with milk according to package directions, stirring with a wire whisk.

STIR in cream cheese, chopped green onions, salt, and pepper until combined. Let stand 5 minutes. Serve potatoes immediately.

freeze unbaked loaves up to 1 month. Thaw in refrigerator overnight, and bake at 350° for 20 minutes. Bake frozen loaves at 350° for 35 minutes. Sprinkle with cheese, and bake 5 more minutes. Let stand 10 minutes before serving. ◆

Slow Cooking for Easy Meals

Solve your supper dilemma with these slow-cooker dishes that practically prepare themselves. Just throw all of the ingredients in, and let the flavors simmer into an almost effortless meal.

BEEF BRISKET

Makes 8 servings
Hands on: 20 min., Hands off: 7 hrs. (HIGH) or 12 hrs. (LOW)

1 (4-pound) beef brisket
$\frac{1}{2}$ teaspoon salt
$\frac{1}{2}$ teaspoon pepper
1 large onion, sliced and separated into rings
$\frac{1}{2}$ cup chili sauce
3 tablespoons brown sugar
2 garlic cloves, pressed
$\frac{1}{2}$ cup light beer
2 tablespoons all-purpose flour
$\frac{1}{4}$ cup water
Black pepper to taste
Garnishes: tomato slices, fresh parsley sprigs

TRIM fat from brisket, and cut brisket into 8 pieces. Sprinkle brisket evenly with salt and pepper.
PLACE onion rings on bottom of a 4$\frac{1}{2}$-quart slow cooker; top with brisket.
COMBINE $\frac{1}{2}$ cup chili sauce and next

Beef Brisket simmers all day in a delicious chili-beer sauce, which is later thickened with flour to make a sumptuous gravy.

3 ingredients; pour over brisket pieces.
COVER and cook on HIGH 5 to 7 hours or on LOW 9 to 12 hours. Remove brisket, reserving liquid in slow cooker.
WHISK together flour and ¼ cup water; add to slow cooker, and whisk constantly 5 minutes or until thickened. Serve over brisket; sprinkle with pepper to taste. Garnish, if desired.

SPICED PORK
Makes 8 servings
Hands on: 20 min., Hands off: 5 hrs. (HIGH) or 10 hrs. (LOW)

1 (2-pound) boneless pork loin roast, trimmed and cut into 2-inch pieces
2 (14.5-ounce) cans diced tomatoes, undrained
1 large onion, chopped
⅓ cup raisins
2 tablespoons tomato paste
2 tablespoons cider vinegar
1 tablespoon chopped pickled jalapeño peppers
1 teaspoon beef bouillon granules
½ teaspoon salt
¼ teaspoon freshly ground pepper
¼ teaspoon ground cinnamon
⅛ teaspoon ground cloves
Hot cooked rice (optional)

PLACE pork in a 4½-quart slow cooker. Add tomatoes and next 10 ingredients, stirring well.
COVER and cook on HIGH 4 to 5 hours or on LOW 8 to 10 hours.
REMOVE pork from slow cooker using a slotted spoon; cool slightly, and shred using 2 forks. Return to slow cooker; cook until thoroughly heated. Serve over hot cooked rice, if desired.

ROAST BEEF WITH HORSERADISH SAUCE
Makes 8 servings
Hands on: 15 min.; Hands off: 4 hrs., 15 min. (HIGH) or 10 hrs., 15 min. (LOW)

SERVE WITH SAUTÉED ONIONS AND PEPPERS AND SWISS CHEESE ON HOAGIE ROLLS FOR A DELICIOUS SANDWICH.

1 teaspoon Creole seasoning
½ teaspoon dried marjoram
¼ teaspoon dried thyme
¼ teaspoon pepper
1 (2¾-pound) eye of round roast, trimmed
3 garlic cloves, cut into 12 pieces
Horseradish Sauce

COMBINE Creole seasoning and next 3 ingredients in a small bowl; rub mixture over entire surface of roast.
CUT 12 (1-inch) slits in roast; stuff each slit with 1 piece of garlic. Place in a 4½-quart slow cooker.
COVER and cook on HIGH 3½ to 4 hours or on LOW 8 to 10 hours. Let stand 15 minutes; cut roast diagonally across the grain into thin slices. Serve with Horseradish Sauce.

Horseradish Sauce:
Makes 1½ cups
Hands on: 5 min.

1 (8-ounce) carton reduced-fat sour cream
½ cup light mayonnaise
1 to 2 tablespoons prepared horseradish
1 garlic clove, pressed

COMBINE all ingredients; cover and chill until ready to serve.

CHUCK ROAST BARBECUE
Makes 6 servings
Hands on: 25 min., Hands off: 6 hrs.

1 (2- to 2½-pound) boneless chuck roast, trimmed
1 medium onion, chopped
¾ cup cola soft drink (not diet)
¼ cup Worcestershire sauce
1 tablespoon cider vinegar
2 garlic cloves, minced
1 teaspoon beef bouillon granules
½ teaspoon dry mustard
½ teaspoon chili powder
¼ teaspoon ground red pepper
½ cup ketchup
2 teaspoons butter
Hamburger buns (optional)

COMBINE roast and chopped onion in a 4-quart slow cooker.
STIR together cola and next 7 ingredients; reserve ½ cup in refrigerator. Pour remaining mixture over roast and onion.
COVER and cook on HIGH 6 hours or until roast is very tender; drain and shred roast. Keep warm.
COMBINE reserved ½ cup cola mixture, ketchup, and butter in a small saucepan; cook over medium heat, stirring constantly, just until thoroughly heated. Pour over shredded roast. Spoon onto hamburger buns, if desired.
NOTE: For testing purposes only, we used Coca-Cola soft drink.

GARDEN CORN SOUP
Makes 8 servings
Hands on: 15 min., Hands off: 5 hrs. (HIGH) or 9 hrs. (LOW)

ADD CHOPPED COOKED CHICKEN OR HAM FOR A HEARTIER MAIN DISH.

1 (16-ounce) package frozen whole kernel corn
2 tablespoons all-purpose flour
1 small onion, chopped
1 medium-size green bell pepper, chopped
2 garlic cloves, pressed
1 (32-ounce) container chicken broth
1 (14.5-ounce) can diced tomatoes
1 vegetable bouillon cube
½ teaspoon dried marjoram
¼ teaspoon dried thyme
¼ teaspoon salt
¼ teaspoon pepper
¼ cup chopped fresh parsley

TOSS corn with flour. Combine corn mixture, chopped onion, and next 9 ingredients in a 4½-quart slow cooker. Cover and cook on HIGH 5 hours or on LOW 9 hours. Stir in parsley before serving.

APPLE CIDER PORK AND VEGETABLES
Makes 4 servings
Hands on: 25 min., Hands off: 8 hrs.

2 small sweet potatoes, peeled and cut into ½-inch-thick slices
1 (6-ounce) package dried mixed fruit
1 medium onion, thinly sliced
1 bay leaf
¾ teaspoon salt
½ teaspoon pepper
½ teaspoon dried rosemary, crushed
1½ pounds lean boneless pork, cut into 1-inch cubes
½ cup all-purpose flour
2 tablespoons vegetable oil
1 cup cider vinegar

PLACE first 7 ingredients in a 4-quart slow cooker.
DREDGE cubed pork in ½ cup flour, and brown in hot oil in a large skillet over medium-high heat. Remove pork, reserving drippings in skillet. Place pork in slow cooker.
ADD cider vinegar to skillet, stirring to loosen any browned particles; pour mixture over pork.
COVER and cook on LOW 6 to 8 hours. Remove and discard bay leaf. ▶

Large sweet onions are slow-cooked until golden brown, adding rich flavor to Caramelized French Onion Soup.

CARAMELIZED FRENCH ONION SOUP

Makes 6 servings
Hands on: 10 min.; Hands off: 2 hrs, 30 min.

THIS MOUTHWATERING SOUP IS TERRIFIC PAIRED WITH A WARM SANDWICH, ESPECIALLY ON A COLD WINTER'S DAY.
TURN TO PAGE 82, AND PICK ONE OF YOUR FAVORITE SANDWICHES.

Caramelized Onions
1 (10.5-ounce) can beef consommé, undiluted
1 (10.5-ounce) can condensed beef broth, undiluted
2 cups water
½ teaspoon dried thyme
¼ cup dry white wine
3 cups large croutons
1 cup (4 ounces) shredded Swiss cheese

COMBINE Caramelized Onions and next 4 ingredients in a 3½-quart slow cooker.

COVER and cook on HIGH 2½ hours or until thoroughly heated. Stir in wine.
LADLE soup into 6 ovenproof bowls, and top evenly with croutons and cheese. Place bowls on a jelly-roll pan.
BROIL 3 inches from heat 5 minutes or until cheese melts. Serve immediately.

Caramelized Onions:
Makes 2 cups
Hands on: 5 min., Hands off: 8 hrs.
2 extra-large sweet onions (about 3 pounds)

1 (10.5-ounce) can condensed chicken or beef broth, undiluted
¼ cup butter

CUT onions in half; cut each half into ½-inch-thick slices.
COMBINE onion slices, broth, and butter in a 3½-quart slow cooker. Cover and cook on HIGH 8 hours or until golden brown and very soft. Store in an airtight container, and chill up to 2 weeks, or, if desired, freeze up to 2 months.

CHICKEN BARBECUE

Makes 8 servings
Hands on: 20 min., Hands off: 4 hrs. (HIGH) or
9 hrs. (LOW)

*COLA SOFT DRINK ADDS SWEETNESS TO
THIS TASTY BARBECUE MIXTURE.*

**3 pounds skinned and boned chicken
    breasts, cut into 2-inch pieces**
1 (18-ounce) bottle barbecue sauce
½ cup cola soft drink (not diet)
1 medium onion, chopped
2 tablespoons lemon juice
2 teaspoons Worcestershire sauce
Hamburger buns (optional)

PLACE chicken in a 4½-quart slow cooker. Add barbecue sauce and next 4 ingredients, stirring well.

COVER and cook on HIGH 4 hours or on LOW 9 hours. Remove chicken from slow cooker; cool slightly, and shred using 2 forks. Return to slow cooker; cook until thoroughly heated. Serve with hamburger buns, if desired.

NOTE: For testing purposes only, we used Coca-Cola soft drink.

WHOLE STUFFED CABBAGE

Makes 6 servings
Hands on: 45 min., Hands off: 6 hrs.

**2 (14.5-ounce) cans whole tomatoes,
    drained and chopped**
1 (6-ounce) can tomato paste
1 tablespoon brown sugar
½ teaspoon Worcestershire sauce
1 large cabbage (about 3½ pounds)
¾ pound ground chuck
1 small onion, chopped
1 garlic clove, pressed
¾ teaspoon salt
½ teaspoon pepper
1 cup cooked long-grain rice
¾ cup water

COMBINE tomatoes, tomato paste, brown sugar, and ½ teaspoon Worcestershire sauce; set aside.

REMOVE and discard any tough outer leaves from cabbage. Carefully remove 2 large outer leaves, and set aside.

CUT out cabbage stem and inner leaves, leaving a 1-inch-thick shell. Set shell aside. Discard cabbage stem, and chop inner leaves, reserving 1 cup. Set aside remaining chopped inner leaves for another use, if desired.

COMBINE 1 cup reserved chopped cabbage, ground chuck, and next 4 ingredients in a large Dutch oven. Cook over medium-high heat 15 minutes or until cabbage is tender, stirring often. Drain and return meat mixture to pan. Stir in 1 cup tomato mixture and rice.

FILL cabbage shell with beef mixture, and cover with reserved large outer leaves, securing with wooden picks. Place in a 5-quart slow cooker; add remaining tomato mixture and ¾ cup water.

COVER and cook on HIGH 6 hours. Remove and discard wooden picks.

CHICKEN AND RICE

Makes 4 servings
Hands on: 25 min., Hands off: 4 hrs.

**1 (10-ounce) package frozen green
    peas, thawed**
4 skinned and boned chicken breasts
½ teaspoon salt
¼ teaspoon pepper
¼ teaspoon paprika
1 medium onion, chopped
1 large green bell pepper, chopped
3 garlic cloves, pressed
**1 (14.5-ounce) can Italian-style
    tomatoes, undrained and chopped**
**1 (5¾-ounce) jar pimiento-stuffed
    olives, drained**
**1 (2-ounce) jar diced pimiento,
    drained**
Hot cooked rice

PLACE peas in a 4- or 5-quart slow cooker. Sprinkle chicken with salt, pepper, and paprika, and place over peas.

ADD onion and next 5 ingredients.
COVER and cook on HIGH 3½ to 4 hours. Serve over rice.

TEXAS STEW

Makes 6 servings
Hands on: 20 min., Hands off: 5 hrs.

*SERVE WITH MEXICAN CORNSTICKS ON
PAGE 57. FOR A SPICIER VERSION OF THIS
STEW, USE MEDIUM OR HOT SALSA.*

**2 pounds beef tips, cut into 1-inch
    pieces**
**1 (14.5-ounce) can Mexican-style
    stewed tomatoes, undrained**
**1 (10.5-ounce) can condensed beef
    broth, undiluted**
**1 (10-ounce) package frozen whole
    kernel corn, thawed**
1 (8-ounce) jar mild salsa
3 carrots, cut into ½-inch slices
**1 medium onion, cut into thin
    wedges**
2 garlic cloves, pressed
1 teaspoon ground cumin
½ teaspoon salt
½ cup water
¼ cup all-purpose flour

COMBINE first 10 ingredients in a 5-quart slow cooker.

COVER and cook on HIGH 3 to 4 hours or until meat is tender.

STIR together ½ cup water and ¼ cup flour until smooth. Stir into meat mixture; cover and cook on HIGH 1 hour or until thickened. ◆

slow-cooker secrets

- Cut large pieces of meat into smaller pieces to fit comfortably into your slow cooker. This will also help ensure that the food is cooked evenly and reaches proper temperatures.
- It's possible to overcook and burn a recipe in a slow cooker, especially because newer models tend to cook hotter. Test for doneness close to the recommended cook time.
- Fill your slow cooker at least half full when following recommended cooking times. Reduce cooking times when using smaller quantities of food.
- Don't remove the lid once you've turned on the cooker; opening the lid allows heat to escape, which increases cooking time.
- Avoid recipes with dairy products, which tend to break down with extended cooking times.
- Change cooking times to fit your schedule. One hour on HIGH typically equals 2 hours on LOW.
- As a general rule, you can adapt a favorite recipe (except soups) so that it can be made in the slow cooker by reducing the amount of liquid by about half.

Sizzle-and-Sear

Chops and Cutlets

Put supper on the table in less than 30 minutes with these low-stress entrées. A hot skillet is your ticket to juicy chops and cutlets. Searing with butter or oil quickly locks in the flavor and gives meat a crispy, golden outside. Try this quick-cooking method for your next meal.

A sauce made of white wine, lemon juice, and skillet drippings is drizzled over Turkey-Basil Piccata.

PARMESAN TURKEY CUTLETS

Makes 4 to 6 servings
Hands on: 25 min.

$\frac{2}{3}$ cup Italian-seasoned breadcrumbs
$\frac{2}{3}$ cup grated Parmesan cheese
1 teaspoon paprika
$\frac{1}{2}$ teaspoon pepper
2 turkey tenderloins (about 1$\frac{1}{2}$ pounds)
Vegetable cooking spray
$\frac{1}{4}$ cup olive oil
Lemon wedges

COMBINE first 4 ingredients; set breadcrumb mixture aside.
CUT tenderloins into 1-inch-thick slices. Place between 2 sheets of heavy-duty plastic wrap, and flatten to $\frac{1}{4}$-inch thickness, using a meat mallet or rolling pin.
COAT both sides of turkey with cooking spray; dredge in breadcrumb mixture.
COOK half of turkey slices in 2 tablespoons hot oil in a large nonstick skillet over medium-high heat 1 minute on each side or until done. Repeat procedure with remaining turkey and hot oil. Serve with lemon wedges.

TURKEY-BASIL PICCATA

Makes 3 to 4 servings
Hands on: 10 min.

2 tablespoons all-purpose flour
$\frac{1}{4}$ teaspoon salt
$\frac{1}{4}$ teaspoon pepper
1 ($\frac{3}{4}$-pound) package turkey cutlets
2 tablespoons olive oil
4 garlic cloves, minced
1$\frac{1}{2}$ teaspoons dried or 1$\frac{1}{2}$ tablespoons chopped fresh basil
$\frac{1}{2}$ cup dry white wine
1$\frac{1}{2}$ tablespoons fresh lemon juice
1 lemon, sliced

COMBINE flour and next 2 ingredients in a shallow dish; dredge turkey cutlets in flour mixture, shaking off excess.
COOK cutlets in hot oil in a large skillet over medium-high heat, 1$\frac{1}{2}$ minutes on each side or until done. Remove from skillet; keep warm.
REDUCE heat to medium-low. Add minced garlic and basil to skillet, and sauté 45 seconds. Add $\frac{1}{2}$ cup white wine, 1$\frac{1}{2}$ tablespoons lemon juice, and lemon slices; cook, stirring to loosen particles from bottom of skillet. Return turkey cutlets to pan; cook just until thoroughly heated. Serve immediately.

CHICKEN SCALOPPINE

Makes 4 servings
Hands on: 10 min.

WINE DEGLAZES THE PAN AND ALSO MAKES A QUICK SAUCE.

½ cup all-purpose flour
1 teaspoon salt
¾ teaspoon seasoned pepper
1½ pounds chicken cutlets
2 tablespoons olive oil
1 cup white wine

COMBINE ½ cup flour, salt, and pepper in a shallow dish; dredge chicken cutlets in flour mixture.

COOK chicken in hot oil in a large skillet over medium-high heat 1 to 2 minutes on each side or until done. Remove from skillet, and keep warm

ADD wine to skillet; cook 1 to 2 minutes or until liquid is reduced by half, stirring to loosen particles from bottom of skillet.

ARRANGE cutlets on a serving platter, and drizzle with wine sauce.

SAUTÉED TURKEY TENDERS

Makes 4 to 6 servings
Hands on: 15 min., Hands off: 15 min.

2 turkey tenderloins (about 1½ pounds)
Salt
Pepper
2 tablespoons olive oil
1 cup dry white wine or chicken broth

SPRINKLE tenderloins with salt and pepper. Cook in hot oil in a large skillet over medium-high heat 5 minutes on each side or until browned. Add wine; reduce heat to medium, and cook 10 to 15 minutes or until done. Cut into slices.

---

make a menu

pork chops
Garlic Mashed Potatoes (page 5)
steamed broccoli or green beans
ice cream with
Hot Fudge Sauce (page 110)

chicken or turkey cutlets
and tenders
Alfredo Sauce (page 48) with hot cooked linguine
Asparagus With
Lemon Butter (page 99)
Watermelon Sorbet (page 106)

Honey-Pecan Pork Chops will hiss as they hit the pan—a telltale sign that the skillet and oil are hot enough.

HONEY-PECAN PORK CHOPS

Makes 4 servings
Hands on: 15 min., Hands off: 7 min.

A SEASONED HONEY-PECAN MIXTURE ADDS CRUNCH AND FLAVOR.

4 (¼-inch-thick) bone-in pork loin chops
¼ cup all-purpose flour
1 tablespoon butter or margarine
¼ cup honey
¼ cup chopped pecans
½ teaspoon Greek seasoning
¼ teaspoon ground red pepper

DREDGE pork chops in flour.

MELT butter in a large skillet over high heat; add pork chops, and cook 4 minutes on each side or until browned. Remove pork chops, and drain on paper towels; keep warm.

STIR together honey and next 3 ingredients; add mixture to skillet. Reduce heat to medium-low; cook, covered, 7 minutes.

SERVE pork chops with sauce.

PAN-FRIED PORK CHOPS

Makes 6 to 8 servings
Hands on: 15 min.

½ cup all-purpose flour
1 teaspoon salt
1 teaspoon seasoned pepper
1½ pounds wafer-thin boneless pork chops
¼ cup vegetable oil

COMBINE ½ cup flour, 1 teaspoon salt, and 1 teaspoon seasoned pepper in a shallow dish; dredge pork chops in flour mixture.

FRY pork chops, in 3 batches, in ¼ cup hot vegetable oil in a large skillet over medium-high heat 1 minute on each side or until browned. Drain pork chops on paper towels. ◆

Chili Night

Chunky Beef 'n' Tomato Chili served with cornbread and shredded cheese makes a hearty meal.

CHUNKY BEEF 'N' TOMATO CHILI

Makes about 6 servings
Hands on: 20 min.; Hands off: 1 hr., 15 min.

1 pound ground round
1 (14.5-ounce) can diced tomatoes
   with green peppers and onions
1 (14.5-ounce) can diced tomatoes
   with zesty mild green chiles
1 (10.5-ounce) can condensed beef broth
2 garlic cloves, pressed
3 tablespoons tomato paste
1 tablespoon chili powder
1 teaspoon ground cumin
½ teaspoon black pepper

½ teaspoon ground red pepper
1 (15-ounce) can light kidney beans,
   rinsed and drained
1 (15-ounce) can dark kidney beans,
   rinsed and drained
Toppings: chipotle hot sauce,
   shredded Cheddar cheese,
   chopped green onions, sour
   cream

COOK 1 pound ground round in a Dutch oven over medium heat, stirring into large chunks, 10 minutes or until beef is no longer pink. (Do not stir beef into crumbles.) Drain and return beef to Dutch oven.

STIR both cans of diced tomatoes and next 7 ingredients into browned beef; reduce heat to medium low, and simmer, uncovered, stirring occasionally, 1 hour. Stir in light and dark kidney beans, and simmer 15 minutes. Serve chili with desired toppings.

Chili is the perfect remedy for cold-weather days. These selections use a variety of beans, meats, and veggies. For a unique serving idea, make Chili in a Biscuit Bowl, and serve it with your favorite toppings.

BLACK BEAN CHILI

Makes 12 cups
Hands on: 35 min.; Hands off: 1 hr., 15 min.

1 pound boneless top sirloin steak, cut into 1-inch cubes
2 large onions, chopped
1 green bell pepper, chopped
1 jalapeño pepper, seeded and chopped
3 to 4 garlic cloves, minced
1½ teaspoons salt, divided
3 tablespoons olive oil
1 (28-ounce) can crushed tomatoes
1 (12-ounce) bottle dark beer
2 tablespoons chili powder
1 tablespoon ground cumin
1 teaspoon sugar
2 teaspoons dried oregano
1½ teaspoons ground black pepper
¼ teaspoon ground red pepper
2 cups beef broth
3 (15-ounce) cans black beans, rinsed and drained
Garnish: shredded Cheddar cheese

COOK first 5 ingredients and ½ teaspoon salt in hot oil in a large Dutch oven over medium-high heat, stirring constantly, 8 minutes or until beef browns and vegetables are tender.
STIR in remaining 1 teaspoon salt, crushed tomatoes, ½ cup beer, and next 6 ingredients; simmer, stirring occasionally, 30 minutes. Stir in remaining 1 cup beer, broth, and beans; simmer, stirring occasionally, 45 minutes or until thoroughly heated. Garnish, if desired.

WHITE BEAN CHILI

Makes 4 quarts
Hands on: 40 min., Hands off: 40 min.

1 medium onion, chopped
1 tablespoon olive oil
2 garlic cloves, minced
8 skinned and boned chicken breasts, cut into bite-size pieces
3 cups water
1 teaspoon salt
2 teaspoons ground cumin
1 teaspoon chili powder

1 teaspoon ground pepper
1 teaspoon dried oregano
4 (15-ounce) cans cannellini or great Northern beans, rinsed, drained, and divided
1 (14½-ounce) can chicken broth
1 (16-ounce) package frozen shoepeg white corn
2 (4.5-ounce) cans chopped green chiles
3 tablespoons lime juice
Garnish: fresh cilantro sprigs

SAUTÉ chopped onion in hot oil in a large Dutch oven over medium-high heat 7 minutes; add minced garlic, and sauté 2 to 3 minutes.
STIR in chicken pieces, and cook, stirring constantly, until chicken is lightly browned. Stir in 3 cups water and next 5 ingredients; reduce heat, and simmer, stirring occasionally, 10 minutes or until chicken is done.
PROCESS 2 cans beans and 1 can broth in a blender until smooth, stopping to scrape down sides.
STIR bean puree, remaining 2 cans of beans, corn, and chiles into chicken mixture in Dutch oven; bring to a boil over medium-high heat. Reduce heat, and simmer, stirring occasionally, 30 minutes or until thoroughly heated. Stir in lime juice just before serving. Garnish, if desired.
NOTE: You may use a handheld submersion blender to puree the beans and broth, if desired. ◆

just add chili

Save your chili leftovers to create more meals later. Freeze up to 1 month, or refrigerate overnight for tomorrow's supper.
■ Top a baked potato with chili, sour cream, and shredded cheese.
■ Jazz up a burger with a heaping dollop of your favorite chili.
■ Grill a meaty quesadilla in the skillet, or spice up a taco with chili.

CHILI IN A BISCUIT BOWL

Makes 6 servings
Hands on: 30 min., Hands off: 35 min

2 cups all-purpose baking mix
⅔ cup milk
½ teaspoon ground red pepper
Vegetable cooking spray
1 pound ground beef
1 medium onion, chopped
1 green bell pepper, chopped
2 (14½-ounce) cans Mexican-style stewed tomatoes, undrained and chopped
1 (15-ounce) can kidney beans, rinsed and drained
2 teaspoons chili powder
Toppings: sour cream, sliced green onions
Garnish: green onions

STIR together first 3 ingredients. Turn dough out onto a surface sprinkled with baking mix. Shape into a ball, and knead 3 to 4 times. Divide into 6 portions.
INVERT 6 (6-ounce) custard cups several inches apart on a lightly greased baking sheet (or use an inverted muffin pan). Coat outsides of cups with cooking spray.
ROLL or pat each dough portion into a 6-inch circle. Place each circle on top of an inverted custard cup; press into a bowl shape.
BAKE at 450° for 10 to 12 minutes. Cool slightly; remove biscuit bowls to a wire rack, and cool completely.
COOK beef, onion, and bell pepper in a Dutch oven over medium heat until meat crumbles and is no longer pink; drain and return to Dutch oven. Stir in tomatoes, beans, and chili powder.
BRING beef mixture to a boil; cover, reduce heat, and simmer 35 minutes. Spoon chili into biscuit bowls, and serve with desired toppings. Garnish, if desired.

Count on Great Chicken

Serve Benne Seed Chicken with Lettuce
Wedge Salad (page 100), Herbed Vegetable
Medley (page 101), cornbread, and sweet tea.

A plate of chicken is always a favorite at the dinner table. Learn how to fry with ease following our basic steps. Or try some simple baked recipes instead, such as flavorful Honey-Pecan Chicken Thighs and roasted Benne Seed Chicken. Either way, you'll know what to serve for supper tonight. Pick up deli sides to have with your chicken, or turn to page 96 for some of our favorites.

CRISPY OVEN-FRIED CHICKEN

Makes 4 to 6 servings
Hands on: 20 min.; Hands off: 8 hrs., 45 min.

1 quart water
1 teaspoon salt
1 (3½-pound) package chicken pieces
½ cup nonfat buttermilk
3 cups crushed cornflakes cereal
2 to 3 teaspoons Creole seasoning
2 teaspoons dried Italian seasoning
½ teaspoon garlic powder
⅛ teaspoon freshly ground black pepper
⅛ teaspoon ground red pepper (optional)

STIR together 1 quart water and 1 teaspoon salt in a large bowl; add chicken. Cover and chill 8 hours.
DRAIN chicken; rinse with cold water, and pat dry. Place chicken in a shallow dish; pour buttermilk over chicken, turning to coat.
COMBINE crushed cereal, next 4 ingredients, and, if desired, ground red pepper in a large zip-top plastic freezer bag. Add chicken to bag, 2 pieces at a time; seal and shake to coat. Place chicken on a lightly greased 15- x 10-inch jelly-roll pan. Repeat with remaining chicken and cereal mixture.
BAKE on lowest oven rack at 400° for 45 minutes or until done. (Do not turn chicken.)

HONEY-PECAN CHICKEN THIGHS

Makes 4 servings
Hands on: 20 min.; Hands off: 2 hrs., 40 min.

CHICKEN THIGHS ARE AS VERSATILE AND CONVENIENT AS CHICKEN BREASTS BUT LOWER IN PRICE. IF YOU CAN'T FIND BONELESS THIGHS AT THE STORE, ASK THE BUTCHER TO REMOVE THE BONES.

½ teaspoon salt
½ teaspoon ground black pepper
½ teaspoon ground red pepper
½ teaspoon dried thyme
8 skinned and boned chicken thighs
¾ cup honey, divided
¾ cup Dijon mustard, divided
2 garlic cloves, minced
1 cup finely chopped pecans
½ teaspoon curry powder
Garnish: flat-leaf parsley sprigs

COMBINE first 4 ingredients; sprinkle evenly over chicken in a shallow dish. Stir together ½ cup honey, ½ cup mustard, and garlic; pour over chicken. Cover and chill 2 hours.
REMOVE chicken from marinade, discarding marinade.
DREDGE chicken in pecans; place on a lightly greased rack in an aluminum foil-lined broiler pan.
BAKE at 375° for 40 minutes or until chicken is done.
STIR together remaining honey, remaining mustard, and ½ teaspoon curry powder; serve sauce with chicken. Garnish, if desired. ▶

BENNE SEED CHICKEN

Makes 4 servings
Hands on: 10 min.; Hands off: 2 hrs., 40 min.

BENNE SEED IS THE SOUTHERN TERM FOR SESAME SEED.

4 chicken leg-thigh quarters (about 2 pounds), separated
1 onion, quartered
2 garlic cloves
1 (1-inch) piece peeled fresh ginger
2 tablespoons sugar
2 teaspoons salt
2 teaspoons ground coriander
1 teaspoon dried crushed red pepper
3 tablespoons lemon juice
3 tablespoons soy sauce
2 tablespoons sesame oil
¼ to ½ cup benne (sesame) seeds

PLACE chicken legs and thighs in a shallow dish or large zip-top plastic freezer bag.
PROCESS onion and next 9 ingredients in a blender or food processor until smooth, stopping to scrape down sides; pour over chicken. Cover or seal, and chill 2 hours.
REMOVE chicken from marinade, discarding marinade. Place chicken in a lightly greased shallow roasting pan. Sprinkle with benne seeds.
BAKE at 375° for 20 minutes on each side or until done.

frying basics

■ Soak chicken in salted water for 8 hours in the refrigerator to prevent excess oil absorption when frying. Drain chicken, and proceed with the recipe as directed.
■ Combine vegetable oil with ¼ cup bacon drippings to add more flavor.
■ Piercing chicken pieces with a fork releases flavorful juices; use tongs to turn during frying.
■ A cast-iron skillet is ideal, but an electric skillet or stainless steel frying pan works just fine. Cast iron, however, offers consistent oil temperature, allowing chicken to cook more evenly, brown better, and get crispier.

Have a down-home plate of fried chicken and fixin's.

ITALIAN-SEASONED FRIED CHICKEN

Makes 4 servings
Hands on: 35 min.

3/4 cup Italian-seasoned breadcrumbs
1/2 cup grated Parmesan cheese
1/4 cup finely chopped fresh parsley
3/4 teaspoon dried oregano
1 large egg
1/2 cup milk
1 tablespoon all-purpose flour
1 (3- to 3 1/2-pound) package chicken
    pieces
Vegetable oil

STIR together Italian-seasoned bread-crumbs and next 3 ingredients. Whisk together egg, 1/2 cup milk, and flour. Dip chicken in egg mixture; dredge in bread-crumb mixture.

POUR oil to a depth of 1 inch in a large heavy skillet; heat oil to 350°. Fry chicken 20 to 25 minutes or until golden, turning occasionally. Drain on paper towels.

SIMPLE FRIED CHICKEN

Makes 8 to 10 servings
Hands on: 30 min.; Hands off: 1 hr., 25 min.

3 cups all-purpose flour
2 teaspoons paprika
1 1/2 teaspoons salt
3 large eggs
1/3 cup milk
2 tablespoons lemon juice
1 (4 1/2-pound) whole chicken, cut up
Vegetable oil

STIR 3 cups flour, 2 teaspoons paprika, and 1 1/2 teaspoons salt in a shallow dish. Whisk together eggs, 1/3 cup milk, and 2 tablespoons lemon juice in a bowl. Dredge

Chilling Simple Fried Chicken before frying adds crispiness to the coating.

chicken in flour mixture; dip in egg mixture. Chill 1 hour.

POUR oil to a depth of 2 inches into a 13-x 9-inch electric skillet; heat to 350°. Fry chicken 10 minutes on each side or until golden brown. Reduce heat to 300°; cover and cook 20 to 25 minutes or until done. Drain on paper towels.

FRIED CHICKEN GRAVY

Makes 1 2/3 cups
Hands on: 15 min.

THIS RICH GRAVY IS EXCELLENT SERVED OVER CREAMY MASHED POTATOES ON PAGE 5.

1 recipe Simple Fried Chicken
1/4 cup all-purpose flour
2 cups milk
1/2 teaspoon salt
1/4 teaspoon pepper

POUR off pan drippings from Simple Fried Chicken, reserving 1/4 cup drippings in electric skillet.

HEAT drippings to 300°. Add 1/4 cup all-purpose flour to drippings, stirring constantly, until browned. Gradually add 2 cups milk to flour mixture; cook, stirring constantly, 3 to 5 minutes or until thickened and bubbly. Stir in salt and pepper. Serve gravy immediately.

HERB-ROASTED CHICKEN THIGHS

Makes 4 servings
Hands on: 15 min.; Hands off: 4 hrs., 25 min.

1/3 cup dry white wine
2 tablespoons chopped fresh chives
1 tablespoon chopped fresh parsley
1 garlic clove, minced
2 tablespoons fresh lemon juice
2 tablespoons olive oil
2 teaspoons Greek seasoning or
    herbes de Provence
1/2 teaspoon salt
1/2 teaspoon pepper
8 skinned and boned chicken thighs

COMBINE white wine and next 8 ingredients in a shallow dish or large zip-top plastic freezer bag; add chicken. Cover or seal, and chill 4 hours.

REMOVE chicken from marinade, discarding marinade. Place chicken on a lightly greased rack in an aluminum foil-lined broiler pan.

BAKE at 400° for 25 minutes or until chicken is done.   ◆

chicken cut up

Cutting your own chicken saves money, and some cooks even believe it tastes better that way. Here's a quick lesson on doing it right.
- Remove the legs by cutting at the joints with a sharp knife.
- Crack the back thigh joint, finding the point with your fingers. Cut straight through to remove the thigh; repeat on the other side. Use kitchen shears to trim extra skin and fat.
- Stretch wings and cut the joints, removing the wings.

- Cut down the back from the tail end to the neck. Clip along the ribs with shears. You'll now have a large breast section.
- Press your fingers on the neck end of the breast; the wishbone connects to these two muscles. You can feel a V-shaped breastbone. Cut straight down from the top of the breast to the cutting board, cutting between the ribs and wishbone from the rest of the breast. Your piece will be V-shaped. Be careful not to crack the bone.

Supper's
on the Stove

Have dinner ready in about an hour with one-dish Shrimp Jambalaya.

These easy meal-in-one dinners make supper a cinch—and cleanup too. From jambalaya to homestyle stew, one pan is all you'll need to get these cozy cooktop meals on the table.

SWEET-AND-SOUR CHICKEN AND RICE

Makes 8 servings
Hands on: 30 min., Hands off: 45 min.

SKINNED AND BONED CHICKEN THIGHS CONTAIN A LITTLE MORE FAT THAN BREAST MEAT, BUT THEY'RE FLAVORFUL, NUTRITIOUS, AND MOIST.

1/2 teaspoon salt
1/2 teaspoon pepper
2 pounds skinned and boned chicken thighs
Vegetable cooking spray
1 small onion, diced
1 medium-size red bell pepper, chopped
2 garlic cloves, minced
1 cup uncooked long-grain rice
1 cup sweet-and-sour dressing
1 cup low-sodium, fat-free chicken broth
2 green onions, chopped

SPRINKLE salt and pepper evenly over chicken thighs. Cook chicken in a Dutch oven coated with cooking spray over medium-high heat 2 to 3 minutes on each side or until browned. Remove chicken from pan, and set aside.
ADD onion, bell pepper, and garlic to Dutch oven coated with cooking spray; sauté 5 minutes. Add rice; sauté 2 minutes or until rice is opaque.
STIR in dressing and broth. Add chicken thighs; bring to a boil. Cover, reduce heat, and simmer 45 minutes or until liquid is absorbed and chicken is done. Sprinkle with green onions.
NOTE: For testing purposes only, we used Old Dutch Sweet & Sour Dressing.

SKILLET BEEF BURGUNDY STEW

Makes 6 servings
Hands on: 30 min., Hands off: 30 min.

1/2 cup all-purpose flour
1 teaspoon salt
1/2 teaspoon pepper
2 pounds boneless sirloin steak, cut into 1-inch cubes
1 medium onion, coarsely chopped
3 tablespoons vegetable oil
6 medium carrots, cut into 1/2-inch-thick slices
1 (10 1/2-ounce) can beef consommé, undiluted
1 (8-ounce) package fresh mushrooms, quartered
1 1/2 cups dry red wine

1 pound small red potatoes, peeled and quartered
1 (1-ounce) envelope dry onion soup mix
1 teaspoon dried thyme

COMBINE first 3 ingredients. Dredge steak cubes in flour mixture.
SAUTÉ steak and onion in hot oil in a Dutch oven 4 to 5 minutes or until steak is browned. Add carrots and remaining ingredients; bring to a boil. Cover, reduce heat, and simmer, stirring occasionally, 30 minutes or until meat and vegetables are tender.

KUNG PAO PORK

Makes 2 to 3 servings
Hands on: 25 min.

3/4 pound lean pork, cut into 1/2-inch cubes
1/4 cup soy sauce, divided
1/4 cup water
2 tablespoons sugar
2 tablespoons lemon juice
2 teaspoons cornstarch
1/4 teaspoon dried crushed red pepper
2 tablespoons olive oil
1 small red bell pepper, cut into 1-inch pieces
1/2 small onion, cut into 1-inch pieces
2 garlic cloves, minced
1/4 cup chopped unsalted dry-roasted peanuts
Hot cooked rice

TOSS together pork and 2 tablespoons soy sauce; set aside.
STIR together remaining 2 tablespoons soy sauce, 1/4 cup water, and next 4 ingredients.
STIR-FRY pork in hot oil in a wok or skillet over medium-high heat 3 minutes or until lightly browned. Add bell pepper, onion, and garlic; stir-fry 3 minutes or until vegetables are tender. Add soy sauce mixture, and stir-fry 2 to 3 minutes or until thickened. Stir in chopped peanuts; serve over rice. ◆

SHRIMP JAMBALAYA

Makes 6 servings
Hands on: 40 min., Hands off: 25 min.

1 pound unpeeled, medium-size fresh shrimp
3 tablespoons vegetable oil
3 tablespoons all-purpose flour
1/2 pound cooked ham, diced
1 medium onion, chopped
1 cup chopped celery
1 cup chopped green bell pepper
4 garlic cloves, minced
2 (14 1/2-ounce) cans chicken broth
1 (14 1/2-ounce) can Cajun-style stewed tomatoes, undrained and chopped
1/4 cup chopped fresh parsley
1 1/2 teaspoons Creole seasoning
1/2 teaspoon ground red pepper
2 cups uncooked long-grain rice

PEEL shrimp, and devein, if desired. Set aside.
STIR together vegetable oil and flour in a Dutch oven; cook over medium-high heat, stirring constantly, 12 to 15 minutes or until roux is caramel-colored.
ADD ham, onion, celery, bell pepper, and garlic cloves, and sauté 7 minutes or until vegetables are tender. Stir in chicken broth, stewed tomatoes, parsley, Creole seasoning, and red pepper; bring to a boil. Stir in rice.
COVER, reduce heat, and simmer 20 minutes or until rice is tender.
STIR in shrimp; cover and cook 5 more minutes or just until shrimp turn pink.

Pizza Tonight

When you're craving pizza, you don't have to wait for delivery. These irresistible recipes can be prepared in less than 30 minutes with the help of store-bought bread, pizza crusts, and sauces. Follow the simple instructions to make these savory pies, or let our ideas inspire you to create your own version.

Roasted Vegetable Pizza is a delicious way to use your favorite produce or last night's leftover veggies.

South-of-the-Border Pizzas

Makes 6 servings
Hands on: 15 min., Hands off: 16 min.

6 (7-inch) pita bread rounds
1 (16-ounce) can fat-free refried beans
1 (4.5-ounce) can chopped green chiles, drained
½ cup diced tomatoes
¼ cup sliced black olives
¾ cup (3 ounces) shredded Mexican four-cheese blend
1½ cups shredded iceberg lettuce
6 tablespoons fat-free sour cream

PLACE pita rounds, slightly overlapping, on a large lightly greased baking sheet.
BAKE at 400° for 4 minutes on each side or until crisp. Cool slightly on a wire rack.
STIR together beans and chiles. Spread ⅓ cup bean mixture over each pita round; sprinkle evenly with tomatoes, olives, and cheese.
BAKE at 400° for 8 minutes or until cheese melts. Top each with ¼ cup lettuce and 1 tablespoon sour cream. Serve immediately.

Hamburger-Mushroom Pizza

Makes 6 servings
Hands on: 15 min., Hands off: 10 min.

6 ounces lean ground beef
1 (16-ounce) unsliced Italian bread loaf
½ cup pizza sauce
8 (⅛-inch-thick) onion slices, separated into rings
1 cup sliced fresh mushrooms
1 teaspoon dried Italian seasoning
½ teaspoon garlic powder
¼ teaspoon dried crushed red pepper
1½ cups (6 ounces) shredded pizza cheese blend

COOK ground beef in a large nonstick skillet over medium-high heat, stirring until it crumbles and is no longer pink. Drain and pat dry with paper towels.
CUT bread in half horizontally. Place both halves, cut side up, on a baking sheet. Spread evenly with pizza sauce, and top with onion slices, mushrooms, and ground beef.
STIR together Italian seasoning, garlic powder, and red pepper; sprinkle over pizzas. Top evenly with shredded cheese.
BAKE at 425° for 10 minutes or until cheese melts. Serve immediately.

Pesto-Tomato Pizza

Makes 4 servings
Hands on: 15 min., Hands off: 10 min.

2 tablespoons commercial pesto
1 (14-ounce) Italian bread shell
¾ pound plum tomatoes, sliced
2 large garlic cloves, thinly sliced
½ cup (2 ounces) shredded mozzarella cheese
⅓ cup shredded Parmesan cheese
1 teaspoon coarsely ground pepper
2 tablespoons shredded fresh basil

SPREAD pesto evenly over bread shell; arrange tomatoes and garlic slices over pesto. Top with cheeses, and sprinkle with pepper.
BAKE on oven rack at 450° for 10 minutes or until cheese melts. Remove from oven; sprinkle with basil. Serve immediately. ◆

Roasted Chicken-and-White Bean Pizzas

Makes 6 servings
Hands on: 20 min., Hands off: 10 min.

1 (16-ounce) can great Northern beans, drained
1 teaspoon lemon juice
⅛ teaspoon garlic powder
⅛ teaspoon pepper
1 cup chopped roasted chicken
¼ teaspoon dried rosemary, crushed
3 (7-inch) pizza crusts
1 cup shredded fresh spinach
¾ cup (3 ounce) shredded sharp provolone cheese

PROCESS great Northern beans and next 3 ingredients in a blender or food processor until smooth, stopping once to scrape down sides.
TOSS together chopped chicken and rosemary.
SPREAD ⅓ cup bean mixture evenly over each pizza crust, and top evenly with chicken mixture, shredded spinach, and shredded cheese.
BAKE on oven rack at 450° for 10 minutes or until crusts are golden. Serve immediately.
NOTE: For testing purposes only, we used Mama Mary's Gourmet Pizza Crusts.

Roasted Vegetable Pizza

Makes 6 servings
Hands on: 25 min., Hands off: 37 min.

1 (10-ounce) can refrigerated pizza crust
1 small sweet onion, cut into thin wedges
1 tablespoon chopped fresh or 1 teaspoon dried thyme
2 tablespoons balsamic vinegar
1 teaspoon olive oil
¼ teaspoon salt
4 small red potatoes, each cut into 8 wedges
4 garlic cloves, thinly sliced
1 small yellow squash, thinly sliced
1 small red bell pepper, cut into 2-inch pieces
1¼ cups (5 ounces) shredded sharp provolone cheese

UNROLL pizza crust on a lightly greased baking sheet; fold edges of dough to form an 11-inch circle.
BAKE at 425° for 7 minutes; set aside.
TOSS together onion, thyme, and next 7 ingredients; spoon into a 13- x 9-inch baking dish.
BAKE vegetable mixture at 500° for 20 minutes, stirring once.
SPRINKLE half of shredded provolone cheese over prepared crust. Top with roasted vegetable mixture, and sprinkle evenly with remaining half of shredded cheese.
BAKE at 425° for 10 minutes or until crust is lightly browned and cheese is melted. Serve immediately.

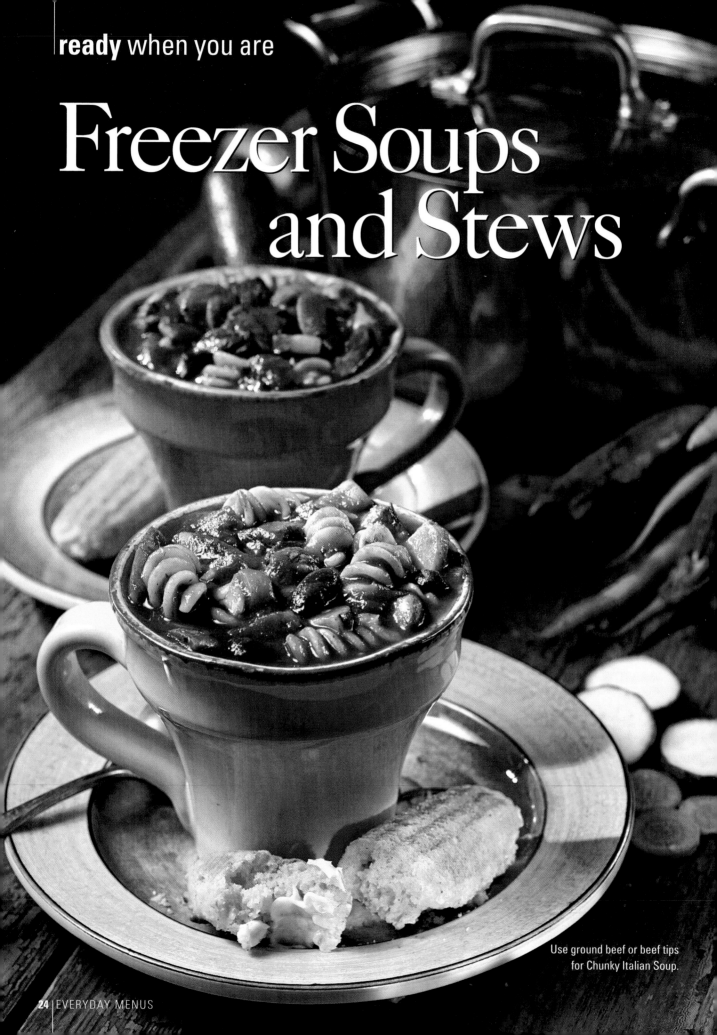

Freezer Soups and Stews

Use ground beef or beef tips for Chunky Italian Soup.

Keep these quick stove-top soups and stews on hand for a meal anytime. Each one doubles easily, allowing you to make freezable batches that you can have on hand for a busy weeknight. Just follow our cooling and freezing tips on page 27; then simply thaw overnight, and reheat for a warm meal in minutes.

COMPANY BEEF STEW

Makes 6 cups
Hands on: 30 min.; Hands off: 2 hrs., 50 min.

1 (3-pound) boneless chuck roast, cut into 1-inch cubes
1 large onion, sliced
1 garlic clove, minced
1 tablespoon dried parsley flakes
1 bay leaf
$\frac{1}{2}$ teaspoon salt
$\frac{1}{2}$ teaspoon pepper
$\frac{1}{2}$ teaspoon dried thyme
1 cup dry red wine
2 tablespoons olive oil
4 bacon slices, cut crosswise into $\frac{1}{4}$-inch pieces
3 tablespoons all-purpose flour
1$\frac{1}{2}$ cups beef broth
$\frac{1}{2}$ pound baby carrots
1 (16-ounce) package frozen pearl onions, thawed
2 tablespoons butter or margarine
1 (8-ounce) package fresh mushrooms

COMBINE first 8 ingredients in a shallow dish or zip-top plastic freezer bag. Combine wine and oil; pour over meat mixture. Cover or seal; chill 1 hour. Drain well, reserving marinade.
COOK bacon in an ovenproof Dutch oven until crisp; remove bacon, reserving drippings in Dutch oven. Drain bacon on paper towels. (If desired, place bacon in a zip-top plastic freezer bag; seal and freeze up to 1 month. Thaw in refrigerator overnight.)
BROWN meat mixture in reserved bacon drippings. Drain and return to Dutch oven. Sprinkle evenly with flour; cook, stirring constantly, 1 to 2 minutes. Add reserved marinade and beef broth; bring to a boil.
BAKE, covered, at 300° for 1 hour and 30 minutes or until tender. Add carrots and onions; bake 30 more minutes.
MELT butter in a large skillet. Add mushrooms; sauté over medium-high heat until tender, and add to meat mixture. (Follow Easy Freezing instructions now, if desired.)
COOK over medium heat in a Dutch oven, stirring occasionally, until thoroughly heated. Sprinkle with bacon.

CHUNKY ITALIAN SOUP

Makes 10 cups
Hands on: 20 min., Hands off: 45 min.

1 pound lean ground beef or beef tips
1 medium onion, chopped
2 (14$\frac{1}{2}$-ounce) cans Italian-style tomatoes
1 (10$\frac{3}{4}$-ounce) can tomato soup, undiluted
4 cups water
2 garlic cloves, minced
2 teaspoons dried basil
2 teaspoons dried oregano
1 teaspoon salt
$\frac{1}{2}$ teaspoon pepper

1 tablespoon chili powder (optional)
1 (16-ounce) can kidney beans, drained
1 (16-ounce) can Italian green beans, drained
1 carrot, chopped
1 zucchini, chopped
8 ounces rotini pasta, cooked
Freshly grated Parmesan cheese (optional)

COOK beef and onion in a Dutch oven over medium heat, stirring until beef crumbles and is no longer pink; drain. Return mixture to pan.
STIR in tomatoes, next 7 ingredients, and, if desired, chili powder; bring to a boil. Reduce heat; simmer, stirring occasionally, 30 minutes. Stir in kidney beans and next 3 ingredients; simmer, stirring occasionally, 15 minutes. Stir in pasta. (Follow Easy Freezing instructions now, if desired.) Sprinkle soup with cheese, if desired.

QUICK CHICKEN AND DUMPLINGS

Makes 4 to 6 servings
Hands on: 10 min., Hands off: 20 min.

4 cups water
3 cups chopped cooked chicken
2 (10$\frac{3}{4}$-ounce) cans cream of chicken soup, undiluted
2 teaspoons chicken bouillon granules
1 teaspoon seasoned pepper
1 (7.5-ounce) can refrigerated buttermilk biscuits

BRING first 5 ingredients to a boil in a Dutch oven over medium-high heat, stirring often.
SEPARATE biscuits in half, forming 2 rounds; cut each round in half. Drop biscuit pieces, 1 at a time, into boiling mixture; stir gently. Cover, reduce heat to low, and simmer, stirring occasionally, 15 to 20 minutes. (Follow Easy Freezing instructions now, if desired.)
LIGHT CHICKEN AND DUMPLINGS: Use reduced-sodium, reduced-fat cream of chicken soup; reduced-fat biscuits; and chopped cooked chicken breasts.

QUICK BEAN SOUP

Makes 10 cups
Hands on: 15 min., Hands off: 10 min.

WITH THREE DIFFERENT KINDS OF BEANS, THIS SOUP IS VERY FILLING.

1 large onion, chopped
1 small green bell pepper, chopped
2 teaspoons vegetable oil
2 (14$\frac{1}{2}$-ounce) cans stewed tomatoes, undrained
1 (16-ounce) can kidney beans, rinsed and drained
1 (15-ounce) can pinto beans, rinsed and drained
1 (15-ounce) can black beans, rinsed and drained
1 (14$\frac{1}{2}$-ounce) can chicken broth
1 cup salsa
1 teaspoon ground cumin

(recipe continues on page 27)

Basil Pesto Toast is a crunchy companion for Roasted Garlic-and-Basil Tomato Soup.

ROASTED GARLIC-AND-BASIL TOMATO SOUP

Makes 4 servings
Hands on: 30 min., Hands off: 15 min.

6 large garlic cloves, slightly flattened
2 (3-ounce) packages shallots, peeled and halved
2 tablespoons olive oil
2 (14½-ounce) cans Italian-style stewed tomatoes
3 cups chicken broth, divided
1 teaspoon hot sauce
1 teaspoon balsamic vinegar
½ teaspoon salt
¼ teaspoon freshly ground black pepper
Pinch of ground red pepper
3 tablespoons minced fresh basil
Basil Pesto Toast (optional)

PLACE garlic and shallots in an 8-inch square pan lined with aluminum foil; drizzle with oil.

BAKE at 450° for 15 minutes, stirring twice; cool slightly.

PROCESS garlic, shallots, tomatoes, 1½ cups chicken broth, and next 5 ingredients, in 2 batches, in a blender or food processor until smooth, stopping to scrape down sides.

COOK tomato mixture and remaining 1½ cups broth in a medium saucepan over medium heat 5 minutes or until thoroughly heated. (Follow Easy Freezing instructions on opposite page now, if desired.) Stir in basil; serve immediately with Basil Pesto Toast, if desired.

Basil Pesto Toast:
Lightly toast 1 French baguette in oven; cut warm bread into thin slices. Spread basil pesto evenly over one side of bread slices. Sprinkle with crumbled tomato-basil feta cheese. Broil bread slices, 3 inches from heat, 1 to 2 minutes or until lightly browned.

SAUTÉ onion and bell pepper in hot oil over medium-high heat in a Dutch oven until tender. Add tomatoes and remaining ingredients; bring to a boil. Cover, reduce heat, and simmer 10 minutes. (Follow Easy Freezing instructions at bottom right now, if desired.)

TURNIP GREENS STEW

Makes 6 to 8 servings
Hands on: 10 min., Hands off: 25 min.

FROZEN SEASONING BLEND IS A MIXTURE OF DICED ONION, RED AND GREEN BELL PEPPERS, AND CELERY. SUBSTITUTE CHOPPED FRESH VEGETABLES, IF DESIRED.

2 cups chopped cooked ham
1 tablespoon vegetable oil
3 cups chicken broth
2 (16-ounce) packages frozen chopped turnip greens
1 (16-ounce) package frozen seasoning blend
1 teaspoon sugar
1 teaspoon seasoned pepper

SAUTÉ chopped ham in hot oil in a Dutch oven over medium-high heat 5 minutes or until lightly browned. Add chicken broth and remaining ingredients; bring mixture to a boil. Cover, reduce heat to low, and simmer, stirring occasionally, 25 minutes. (Follow Easy Freezing instructions at bottom right now, if desired.)
NOTE: For testing purposes only, we used McKenzie's Seasoning Blend.
COLLARD STEW: Omit turnip greens. Sauté ham as directed. Add 1 (16-ounce) package frozen chopped collard greens, chicken broth, and remaining ingredients; bring to a boil. Cover, reduce heat to low, and simmer, stirring occasionally, 15 minutes. Add 1 (16-ounce) can black-eyed peas, drained; cook 10 minutes.

TACO SOUP

Makes 10 cups
Hands on: 15 min., Hands off: 30 min.

1 pound ground beef
1 (15.5-ounce) can pinto beans, rinsed and drained
1 (15.5-ounce) can whole kernel corn, rinsed and drained
1 (14.5-ounce) can green beans, rinsed and drained
1 (15-ounce) can ranch beans, undrained
1 (14.5-ounce) can stewed tomatoes
1 (12-ounce) can beer
1 (10-ounce) can diced tomatoes and green chiles
1 (1¼-ounce) envelope taco seasoning mix
1 (1-ounce) envelope Ranch dressing mix
5 (6-inch) corn tortillas
Vegetable cooking spray
Salt

BROWN ground beef in a stockpot, stirring until it crumbles and is no longer pink; drain. Return beef to pot. Stir in pinto beans and next 8 ingredients; bring to a boil. Reduce heat; simmer 30 minutes. (Follow Easy Freezing instructions below now, if desired.)
CUT tortillas into ¼-inch strips. Place on baking sheet; coat tortillas with cooking spray, and sprinkle with salt.
BAKE at 400° for 5 to 8 minutes. Ladle soup into bowls, and top with corn tortilla strips.

SAUSAGE, SPINACH, AND BEAN SOUP

Makes about 10 cups
Hands on: 25 min.

1 (8-ounce) package ground Italian sausage
1 teaspoon olive oil
5 garlic cloves, minced
½ teaspoon dried crushed red pepper
2 (10-ounce) packages fresh spinach, torn
2 (15-ounce) cans cannellini beans, undrained
3 cups chicken broth
¼ cup butter
½ cup freshly shredded Parmesan cheese
2 plum tomatoes, diced
2 tablespoons chopped fresh parsley
¼ teaspoon salt
¼ teaspoon pepper

BROWN Italian sausage in hot oil in a Dutch oven over medium-high heat 10 minutes, stirring until it crumbles and is no longer pink. Add minced garlic and crushed red pepper, and sauté 2 minutes. Add spinach, and sauté 2 minutes or until wilted.
STIR in cannellini beans, and cook 1 minute. Add 3 cups chicken broth, and bring to a boil. Add ¼ cup butter, shredded Parmesan cheese, diced tomatoes, and 1 tablespoon chopped parsley; cook until thoroughly heated. Stir in salt and pepper. (Follow Easy Freezing instructions below now, if desired.) Sprinkle warm soup evenly with remaining 1 tablespoon chopped parsley.

EASY BRUNSWICK STEW

Makes 14 cups
Hands on: 15 min.; Hands off: 6 hrs., 30 min.

1 large onion, chopped
1 celery rib, chopped
1 large green bell pepper, chopped
1 cup frozen okra, thawed
4 cups frozen cubed hash browns, thawed
¾ cup barbecued pork, chopped
1 cup chopped cooked chicken
1 (14½-ounce) can diced tomatoes, undrained
1 (15-ounce) can tomato sauce
1 (15¼-ounce) can whole kernel corn with red and green peppers, drained
1 (15¼-ounce) can lima beans, drained
2 cups chicken broth
½ teaspoon salt
½ teaspoon pepper
¼ teaspoon Worcestershire sauce

COMBINE onion and remaining ingredients in a 5-quart slow cooker. Cook, covered, at HIGH 6 hours and 30 minutes. (Follow Easy Freezing instructions below now, if desired.) ▶

easy freezing

Make sure you let hot food cool before freezing. Pour hot soup into a large pan or baking dish; cool slightly. Spoon cooled soup into freezer-safe containers, or use small zip-top plastic freezer bags for individual portions. Cover or seal, and freeze up to 1 month. Thaw overnight in the refrigerator, and reheat.
Note: Each of the soups shown here is ready to be frozen at a different stage of preparation; see individual recipes.

CHICKEN NOODLE SOUP

Makes 9 cups
Hands on: 30 min., Hands off: 10 min.

½ cup butter or margarine
2 medium carrots, chopped
2 medium parsnips, chopped
1 medium-size sweet onion, diced
1 large celery rib, chopped
4 skinned and boned chicken breasts,
   cut into 1-inch pieces
¼ cup all-purpose flour
¼ teaspoon pepper
5 cups chicken broth
4 ounces uncooked wide egg noodles
2 tablespoons chopped fresh parsley

MELT butter in a large Dutch oven over medium-high heat. Add carrots and next 3 ingredients; sauté 5 minutes. Add chicken, and sauté 5 minutes. Add flour and pepper, stirring until blended. Cook 1 minute, stirring constantly. Add broth; bring to a boil over medium-high heat, stirring constantly. Add noodles; return to a boil. Reduce heat, and simmer, stirring occasionally, 10 minutes. Stir in parsley. (Follow Easy Freezing instructions on previous page now, if desired.)

A fresh lemon slice and basil sprig float atop Tomato-Basil Cream Soup.

TOMATO-BASIL CREAM SOUP

Makes 6½ cups
Hands on: 40 min.; Hands off: 1 hour, 10 min.

4 shallots, diced
2 garlic cloves, pressed
1 celery rib, chopped
½ pound leeks, chopped
2 tablespoons oil
2 (14½-ounce) cans Italian-style tomatoes, undrained and chopped
1 tablespoon dried basil
2 (14-ounce) cans chicken broth
¼ teaspoon salt
1 cup whipping cream
Garnishes: lemon slices, fresh basil sprigs

COOK first 4 ingredients in hot oil in a Dutch oven over low heat, stirring often, 10 to 12 minutes or until tender. (Do not brown.) Add tomatoes and basil; cook over medium heat, stirring occasionally, 10 minutes. Add broth and salt; bring to a boil. Reduce heat, and simmer, stirring occasionally, 1 hour. Cool.

PROCESS mixture, in batches, in a food processor or blender until smooth, stopping to scrape down sides. (Follow Easy Freezing instructions on page 27 now, if desired.)

HEAT in Dutch oven over medium heat. Stir in 1 cup whipping cream; cook, stirring constantly, until thoroughly heated. (Do not boil.) Garnish, if desired.

CREAM OF REUBEN SOUP

Makes 12 cups
Hands on: 20 min., Hands off: 25 min.

IF YOU CHOOSE TO FREEZE THIS RECIPE, BE SURE TO RETURN THAWED SOUP MIXTURE TO A DUTCH OVEN TO REHEAT.

6 cups chicken broth
¾ pound cooked corned beef, chopped
1 (10-ounce) can chopped sauerkraut, drained
1 large carrot, grated
1 small onion, chopped
1 garlic clove, minced
½ teaspoon dried thyme
¼ teaspoon ground white pepper
¼ teaspoon dried tarragon
1 bay leaf
3 tablespoons cornstarch
⅓ cup cold water
2 cups (8 ounces) shredded Swiss cheese
1 cup whipping cream
Rye bread cubes, toasted

BRING 6 cups chicken broth and next 9 ingredients to a boil in a Dutch oven over medium heat; reduce heat, and simmer 25 minutes. Remove and discard bay leaf.

STIR together 3 tablespoons cornstarch and ⅓ cup cold water, and stir into soup mixture. Bring to a boil over medium-high heat; boil, stirring constantly, 1 minute. Remove soup mixture from heat. (Follow Easy Freezing instructions on page 27 now, if desired.)

ADD 2 cups shredded Swiss cheese and 1 cup whipping cream, stirring until cheese melts. Top each serving with toasted rye bread cubes. ◆

Start with Ham

A mixture of pineapple juice, fresh ginger, and garlic serves as a basting sauce for Pineapple-Glazed Ham.

PINEAPPLE-GLAZED HAM

Makes 14 to 16 servings
Hands on: 30 min.; Hands off: 2 hrs., 45 min.

EVEN THOUGH IT TECHNICALLY DOESN'T REQUIRE ADDITIONAL COOKING, REHEATING A FULLY COOKED HAM MAXIMIZES THE FLAVOR.

4 cups pineapple juice
1 (1-inch) piece fresh ginger, peeled
   and sliced
4 garlic cloves, pressed
1 (7- to 9-pound) bone-in smoked fully
   cooked ham
12 to 16 whole cloves
¼ cup Dijon mustard
1 cup firmly packed brown sugar
1 (20-ounce) can pineapple slices in
   juice, drained (optional)
10 maraschino cherries, halved
   (optional)

STIR together first 3 ingredients in a saucepan; bring to a boil. Reduce heat to medium low, and simmer 25 minutes or until liquid is reduced by half. Pour mixture through a wire-mesh strainer into a bowl, discarding solids. Set pineapple juice mixture aside.

REMOVE skin and excess fat from ham. Make ¼-inch-deep cuts in a diamond design, and insert cloves at 1-inch intervals. Place ham in an aluminum foil-lined roasting pan. Spread mustard evenly over ham.

PAT brown sugar on top of mustard. Pour pineapple juice mixture into pan.

ARRANGE pineapple slices and maraschino cherries evenly over ham, if desired; secure with wooden picks.

BAKE at 325° for 1 hour. Remove ham from oven; shield with aluminum foil to prevent excess browning, and bake an additional 1 to 1½ hours or until a meat thermometer inserted into thickest portion registers 140°, basting every 30 minutes with pan juices. Let stand 15 minutes before slicing.

REMOVE from pan, reserving drippings. Cover ham, and chill, if desired. Chill reserved drippings.

REMOVE and discard fat from drippings. Bring drippings to a boil in a small saucepan. Serve warm with ham.

With one basic ham recipe, you can plan a variety of meals. Prepare the ham as directed, and serve the oven-baked slices with favorite side dishes (see recipes on pages 96 and 102). Then save leftovers to make a variety of tasty dishes from Ham Spaghetti to Ham-and-Roasted Vegetable Salad With Honey-Mustard Vinaigrette. Whether you're craving a stuffed potato or need a quick casserole, ham is an easy dinner solution.

HAM-BROCCOLI POT PIE

Makes 6 servings
Hands on: 20 min., Hands off: 35 min.
1 (10-ounce) package frozen chopped broccoli, thawed
1 (11-ounce) can sweet whole kernel corn, drained
1 (10³/₄-ounce) can cream of mushroom soup, undiluted
2 cups diced cooked ham
2 cups (8 ounces) shredded colby-Jack cheese blend
1 (8-ounce) container sour cream
¹/₂ teaspoon pepper
¹/₂ teaspoon dried mustard
¹/₂ (15-ounce) package refrigerated piecrusts

ARRANGE chopped broccoli in a lightly greased 11- x 7-inch baking dish.
STIR together corn and next 6 ingredients. Spoon over broccoli.
UNROLL piecrust; pat or roll into an 11- x 7-inch rectangle, and place over ham mixture. Crimp edges, and cut 4 slits for steam to escape.
BAKE at 400° for 30 to 35 minutes or until crust is golden.

FRENCH MARKET SANDWICHES

Makes 4 servings
Hands on: 15 min., Hands off: 15 min.
1 (14-ounce) can artichoke hearts, drained and chopped
1 cup (4 ounces) shredded Swiss cheese
³/₄ cup shredded Parmesan cheese
¹/₄ cup mayonnaise
7 green onions, sliced
3 tablespoons sweet hot mustard
8 ounces sliced cooked ham
4 large croissants, split

STIR together chopped artichoke hearts and next 5 ingredients.
PLACE ham slices on bottom halves of croissants. Spoon artichoke mixture evenly over ham. Cover with top halves of croissants. Place sandwiches on a baking sheet.
BAKE at 350° for 12 to 15 minutes or until thoroughly heated.
NOTE: For testing purposes only, we used Woeber's Sweet and Spicy Mustard.

HAM SPAGHETTI

Makes 10 to 12 servings
Hands on: 15 min., Hands off: 30 min.
16 ounces uncooked vermicelli
1 large sweet onion, diced
1 large green bell pepper, diced
4 cups chopped cooked ham
2 tablespoons vegetable oil
2 (10³/₄-ounce) cans cream of mushroom soup, undiluted*
1 (16-ounce) container sour cream*
1 (16-ounce) loaf pasteurized prepared cheese product, cubed*

¹/₂ teaspoon pepper
¹/₂ cup (2 ounces) shredded Cheddar cheese
COOK pasta according to package directions; drain.
SAUTÉ onion, bell pepper, and 4 cups chopped ham in hot oil in a large skillet over medium-high heat 6 to 8 minutes or until vegetables are tender. Stir in cream of mushroom soup and next 3 ingredients. Cook over medium heat, stirring constantly, 4 to 5 minutes or until cheese product is melted. Stir in pasta; spoon mixture into a lightly greased 13- x 9-inch baking dish. Sprinkle with ¹/₂ cup Cheddar cheese.
BAKE at 350° for 30 minutes or until hot and bubbly.
*Reduced-sodium, reduced-fat cream of mushroom soup; light sour cream; and light pasteurized prepared cheese product may be substituted.
NOTE: For testing purposes only, we used Velveeta pasteurized prepared cheese product. ▶

carving clues

Carving ham is a cinch. A sharp carving knife, a meat fork, and these simple instructions are all you need for the job.
Hold the knife perpendicular to the bone. Cut full slices just until you feel the knife is touching the bone. Then place your knife at a 90-degree angle to the slices, parallel to the bone, and cut to release the slices. Once all the meat has been cut from this side, turn the ham over, and repeat the procedure.

DOUBLE-STUFFED HAM-AND-BROCCOLI POTATOES

Makes 8 servings
Hands on: 25 min.; Hands off: 1 hr., 30 min.

6 (10-ounce) baking potatoes*
2 cups chopped cooked ham
1 (10-ounce) package frozen chopped
    broccoli, thawed and drained
1 (8-ounce) container soft chive-and-
    onion cream cheese
1 teaspoon garlic salt
½ teaspoon freshly ground black
    pepper
½ cup (2 ounces) shredded Cheddar
    cheese

PIERCE potatoes with a fork, and bake at 450° for 1 hour or until tender. Let potatoes cool to touch.

CUT potatoes in half lengthwise, and scoop out pulp, leaving 8 (¼-inch-thick) shells intact; reserve remaining 4 shells for another use, if desired.

STIR together potato pulp, ham, and next 4 ingredients until blended. Spoon mixture evenly into 8 potato shells. Sprinkle with ½ cup shredded Cheddar cheese.

Place stuffed potatoes on a baking sheet. BAKE at 350° for 25 to 30 minutes or until cheese is melted.

*1 (22-ounce) package frozen mashed potatoes may be substituted for baking potatoes. Prepare mashed potatoes according to package directions. Stir in ham and next 4 ingredients. Spoon into a lightly greased 11- x 7-inch baking dish; sprinkle with shredded Cheddar cheese. Bake as directed.

Ham-and-Bean Chowder

Makes 12 to 16 servings
Hands on: 45 min.

PINQUITOS ARE SMALL PINTO BEANS. FREEZE THE CHOWDER LEFTOVERS, AND REHEAT FOR A COMFORTING MEAL IN MINUTES.

3 cups chopped cooked ham
2 celery ribs, diced
2 carrots, diced
2 garlic cloves, minced
1 large sweet onion, diced
2 tablespoons olive oil
3 (16-ounce) cans cannellini beans, drained*
1 (32-ounce) container chicken broth
1 (24-ounce) package frozen hash browns with onions and peppers, thawed
1 (16-ounce) can black beans, drained
1 (16-ounce) can pinquitos, drained
2 (4.5-ounce) cans chopped green chiles
½ teaspoon garlic salt
½ teaspoon ground red pepper
½ teaspoon ground black pepper

SAUTÉ 3 cups chopped ham and next 4 ingredients in hot oil in an 8-quart stockpot over medium-high heat 6 to 8 minutes or until tender.

PROCESS 2 cans cannellini beans and 2 cups chicken broth in a blender until smooth, stopping to scrape down sides. Add to ham mixture. Stir in remaining can of cannellini beans, remaining 2 cups chicken broth, hash browns, and remaining ingredients.

COOK over medium heat, stirring often, 20 to 25 minutes or until thoroughly heated.

*3 (16-ounce) cans Great Northern beans may be substituted.

Ham-and-Pasta Salad

Makes 4 servings
Hands on: 20 min.

8 ounces penne pasta, cooked
1½ cups diced ham
1 cup Ranch dressing
4 green onions, sliced
2 tablespoons chopped fresh parsley
2 tablespoons chopped fresh basil
1 garlic clove, minced
¼ teaspoon freshly ground black pepper

TOSS together cooked pasta and remaining ingredients. Serve immediately.

Ham adds a smoky flavor to Grits and Greens.

Grits and Greens

Makes 6 servings
Hands on: 45 min.

1 (16-ounce) package fresh collard greens
4 cups chicken broth, divided
1 cup whipping cream
1 cup uncooked stone-ground or regular grits
¼ to ½ cup milk
¼ cup butter
1½ cups freshly grated Parmesan cheese
¼ teaspoon freshly ground pepper
2 cups cubed cooked ham

COMBINE collard greens and 1 cup chicken broth in a large skillet; bring to a boil. Cover, reduce heat, and simmer 5 minutes or until tender. Drain collard greens, and plunge into ice water to stop the cooking process. Drain well on paper towels; set aside.

BRING whipping cream and remaining 3 cups chicken broth to a boil in a large saucepan; gradually stir in grits. Return to a boil over medium heat; cover, reduce heat, and simmer, stirring often, 25 to 30 minutes. Gradually add milk, as necessary, for desired consistency.

ADD butter, cheese, and pepper to grits, stirring until butter and cheese melt. Stir in greens and ham. Cook, stirring constantly, until thoroughly heated.

Ham-and-Roasted Vegetable Salad With Honey-Mustard Vinaigrette

Makes 6 servings
Hands on: 25 min., Hands off: 30 min.

3 cups diced cooked ham
1 pound small new potatoes, halved
1 large red bell pepper, cut into 2-inch pieces
1 large sweet onion, cut into 2-inch pieces
2 tablespoons olive oil
½ teaspoon garlic salt
½ teaspoon freshly ground pepper
9 cups mixed salad greens
Honey-Mustard Vinaigrette

TOSS together first 7 ingredients in a lightly greased 15- x 10-inch jelly-roll pan.

BAKE mixture at 450° for 30 minutes or until roasted.

TOSS together salad greens and Honey-Mustard Vinaigrette. Top with ham mixture.

Honey-Mustard Vinaigrette:

Makes 1 cup
Hands on: 5 min.

¼ cup spicy brown mustard
¼ cup honey
3 tablespoons cider vinegar
¼ teaspoon salt
¼ teaspoon freshly ground pepper
½ cup olive oil

WHISK together first 5 ingredients. Gradually whisk in oil.

▶

Keep supper simple with Creamy Ham Casserole and a green salad or vegetable dish.

CREAMY HAM CASSEROLE

Makes 6 servings
Hands on: 25 min., Hands off: 45 min.

- **3 cups cauliflower florets (about 1 medium cauliflower)**
- **4 tablespoons butter or margarine**
- **1/3 cup all-purpose flour**
- **1 cup milk**
- **1 cup (4 ounces) shredded Cheddar cheese**
- **1/2 cup sour cream**
- **2 cups cubed cooked ham**
- **1 (3-ounce) can sliced mushrooms, drained**
- **1 cup soft breadcrumbs**
- **1 tablespoon cold butter or margarine**

COOK 3 cups cauliflower florets in boiling salted water to cover 10 to 12 minutes or until tender; drain and set aside.

MELT 4 tablespoons butter in a medium saucepan over medium-high heat. Whisk in 1/3 cup flour until smooth. Gradually add 1 cup milk, whisking constantly, until mixture begins to thicken. Add shredded Cheddar cheese and 1/2 cup sour cream, stirring until cheese melts. (Do not boil.)

STIR cauliflower, ham, and mushrooms into cheese sauce; pour into a 2-quart baking dish. Sprinkle breadcrumbs evenly over casserole. Cut 1 tablespoon butter into pieces, and sprinkle evenly over breadcrumbs.

BAKE at 350° for 45 minutes or until golden and bubbly.

CHEDDAR-CHILI CHEESECAKE

Makes 6 to 8 servings
Hands on: 25 min.; Hands off: 1 hr., 30 min.

- **1/4 cup fine, dry breadcrumbs**
- **1/4 cup (1 ounce) shredded sharp Cheddar cheese**
- **3 (8-ounce) packages cream cheese, softened**
- **12 thin slices cooked ham, diced and divided**
- **1 (10-ounce) block sharp Cheddar cheese, shredded**
- **5 green onions, chopped**
- **3 large eggs**
- **2 small jalapeño peppers, minced**
- **1 clove garlic, minced**
- **1 cup sour cream**
- **2 tablespoons milk**
- **Crackers**

STIR together breadcrumbs and ¼ cup shredded cheese; sprinkle on bottom of a buttered 9-inch springform pan. Set aside.

BEAT cream cheese at medium speed with an electric mixer; add half of ham, shredded cheese, and next 6 ingredients, beating at low speed until well blended.

POUR half of cream cheese mixture into prepared pan; top with remaining ham. Pour remaining mixture over ham.

BAKE at 325° for 1 hour or until center is set. Let stand 30 minutes. Gently run a knife around the edge of cheesecake, and release sides. Serve slightly warm or at room temperature with crackers.

QUICK FIESTA QUESADILLAS

Makes 4 to 6 servings
Hands on: 25 min.

1½ cups diced cooked ham
3 plum tomatoes, seeded and chopped
1 cup crumbled goat cheese
½ medium-size red onion, diced
¼ cup chopped fresh cilantro
¼ cup lime juice
¼ cup (2 ounces) cream cheese, softened
1 (4.5-ounce) can chopped green chiles, drained
6 (8-inch) flour tortillas
Vegetable cooking spray

COMBINE first 8 ingredients. Spread 1 side of each tortilla with about ½ cup ham mixture; fold tortillas in half.

COOK tortillas, in batches, in a nonstick skillet coated with cooking spray over medium-high heat 1 minute on each side or until golden brown. Serve immediately.

HAM PASTA CASSEROLE

Makes 6 to 8 servings
Hands on: 25 min., Hands off: 25 min.

2 (7-ounce) packages thin spaghetti, uncooked*
¼ cup butter or margarine
1 (8-ounce) package sliced fresh mushrooms
6 green onions, chopped
3 garlic cloves, minced
½ teaspoon salt
½ teaspoon pepper
3 tablespoons all-purpose flour
2 cups half-and-half or whipping cream
2 cups (8 ounces) shredded Cheddar cheese
½ cup shredded Parmesan cheese
2 cups chopped cooked ham

COOK pasta according to package directions. Drain and set aside.

MELT ¼ cup butter in a large skillet over medium-high heat; add sliced mushrooms, chopped green onions, and minced garlic; sauté 3 to 4 minutes or until tender. Add salt and pepper.

WHISK in flour gradually until blended. Gradually whisk in half-and-half until smooth. Stir in Cheddar cheese and ¼ cup Parmesan cheese until melted; stir in ham and pasta. Pour mixture into a lightly greased 13- x 9-inch baking dish. Sprinkle with remaining ¼ cup Parmesan cheese.

BAKE at 350° for 20 to 25 minutes.

*1 (12-ounce) package thin egg noodles may be substituted for spaghetti. Cook according to package directions.

EASY CHICKEN CORDON BLEU

Makes 6 servings
Hands on: 20 min., Hands off: 25 min.

½ teaspoon salt
¼ teaspoon pepper
6 skinned and boned chicken breasts
1 (5.5-ounce) box seasoned croutons, crushed
⅓ cup shredded Parmesan cheese
2 egg whites
2 tablespoons water
12 thinly sliced smoked ham slices
6 Swiss cheese slices
Honey mustard dressing (optional)

SPRINKLE salt and pepper evenly over chicken; set aside.

COMBINE crouton crumbs and shredded Parmesan cheese in a large zip-top plastic bag. Whisk together egg whites and 2 tablespoons water in a shallow bowl.

DIP chicken in egg white mixture, and drain. Place 1 breast in bag; seal and shake to coat. Remove to a lightly greased aluminum foil-lined baking sheet, and repeat with remaining chicken.

BAKE at 450° for 20 minutes or until chicken is done. Top each breast with 2 ham slices and 1 Swiss cheese slice. Bake 5 more minutes or until cheese melts. Serve with honey mustard dressing, if desired.

FRIED RICE

Makes 4 servings
Hands on: 35 min.

¼ cup vegetable oil, divided
2 large eggs
1 cup diced cooked ham
½ large red bell pepper, diced
½ large sweet onion, diced
½ cup frozen sweet green peas, thawed
3 cups cooked rice
¼ cup soy sauce
1 teaspoon chili-garlic sauce
4 green onions, sliced

HEAT 1 tablespoon oil in a skillet or wok at medium-high heat 2 minutes. Add eggs, and cook 1 minute on each side. Remove from skillet; chop eggs, and set aside.

HEAT remaining 3 tablespoons oil in skillet or wok; add ham, and stir-fry 1 to 2 minutes or until golden. Add bell pepper and onion; stir-fry 5 minutes. Add peas and next 3 ingredients; stir-fry 3 to 4 minutes or until thoroughly heated.

STIR in cooked eggs, and sprinkle with green onions.   ◆

ham 101

- Fully cooked ham: Can be eaten cold, although heating it to an internal temperature of 140° brings out the full flavor.
- Ham labeled "cook before eating": Must reach 160° internally before serving.
- Bone-in ham: Available whole, butt end, or shank end only.
- Boneless ham: The ham is rolled or packed in casing after removing the bone.
- Country ham: Prepared with a dry-rub cure. Most country hams are very dry and salty and require soaking before cooking.
- Dry-cured ham: Rubbed with a mixture of salt, sugar, nitrates, and seasonings, and then air-dried.
- Prosciutto: Seasoned, salt-cured, and then air-dried. Italy's Parma ham is a true prosciutto. It's usually sold thinly sliced and served as an appetizer.
- Smoked ham: Hung in a smokehouse to take on the smoky flavor of the wood used.

Make-Ahead Casseroles

Busy weeknights require fast meals, and these hearty casseroles guarantee fuss-free suppers. They're also great for drop-in company. Prepare as directed, and freeze the unbaked casserole up to 1 month, or refrigerate it overnight. For best results, let the casserole stand at room temperature for 30 minutes before baking.

Don't let cannelloni shells intimidate you—use our easy stuffing technique.

CHICKEN CANNELLONI WITH ROASTED RED BELL PEPPER SAUCE

Makes 6 to 8 servings
Hands on: 30 min., Hands off: 30 min.

FOR EASY FREEZING, PREPARE AND STUFF UNBAKED CANNELLONI SHELLS. WRAP EACH SHELL TIGHTLY IN WAX PAPER, AND FREEZE UNTIL READY TO SERVE. LET THAW IN THE REFRIGERATOR. UNWRAP AND PLACE IN A BAKING DISH; TOP WITH YOUR FAVORITE SUPERMARKET PASTA SAUCE OR OUR ROASTED RED BELL PEPPER SAUCE, AND BAKE AS DIRECTED.

1 (8-ounce) package cannelloni or manicotti shells
4 cups finely chopped cooked chicken
2 (8-ounce) containers chive-and-onion cream cheese
1 (10-ounce) package frozen chopped spinach, thawed and well drained
1 cup (4 ounces) shredded mozzarella cheese
½ cup Italian-seasoned breadcrumbs
¾ teaspoon garlic salt
1 teaspoon seasoned pepper
Roasted Red Bell Pepper Sauce
Garnish: chopped fresh basil or parsley

COOK pasta according to package directions; drain and set aside.
STIR together chicken and next 6 ingredients in a large bowl.
CUT 1 side of pasta shells lengthwise, opening each shell.
SPOON ½ cup chicken mixture into each shell, gently pressing cut sides together. Place shells, seam side down, in 2 lightly greased 11- x 7-inch baking dishes.
POUR Roasted Red Bell Pepper Sauce evenly over shells.
BAKE, covered, at 350° for 25 to 30 minutes or until thoroughly heated. Garnish, if desired.

Roasted Red Bell Pepper Sauce:
Makes 3½ cups
Hands on: 5 min.

SAVOR THIS RICH SAUCE OVER YOUR FAVORITE PASTA OR GRILLED MEATS.

2 (7-ounce) jars roasted red bell peppers, drained
1 (16-ounce) jar creamy Alfredo sauce
1 (3-ounce) package shredded Parmesan cheese

PROCESS all ingredients in a blender until smooth, stopping occasionally to scrape down sides.
NOTE: For testing purposes only, we used Bertolli Creamy Alfredo sauce.

Veggie Mac-and-Cheese

Makes 6 to 8 servings
Hands on: 45 min., Hands off: 35 min.

8 ounces uncooked elbow macaroni
1 cup chopped fresh broccoli
1 cup diced yellow squash
½ cup diced carrot
1 small red onion, diced
2 garlic cloves, minced
2 teaspoons olive oil
1 (7-ounce) jar roasted red bell
**   peppers, drained and diced**
1 (16-ounce) container ricotta cheese
1 (12-ounce) can evaporated milk
1 tablespoon Dijon mustard
1 teaspoon salt
1 teaspoon freshly ground pepper
2 large eggs, lightly beaten
3 plum tomatoes, sliced
⅓ cup Italian-seasoned breadcrumbs
½ cup (2 ounces) shredded Romano
**   cheese**

COOK macaroni in a Dutch oven according to package directions; drain.

SAUTÉ broccoli and next 4 ingredients in hot oil in Dutch oven over medium heat 3 to 4 minutes or until tender. Remove from heat; add macaroni, bell peppers, and next 5 ingredients, stirring until blended. Stir in beaten eggs.

POUR mixture into a lightly greased 13- x 9-inch baking dish. (If desired, cover and chill 8 hours, or freeze up to 1 month; thaw in refrigerator overnight. Let stand at room temperature 30 minutes before baking.) Top with tomato slices; sprinkle with Italian-seasoned breadcrumbs and Romano cheese.

BAKE, covered, at 350° for 15 minutes; uncover and bake 20 more minutes or until golden. Serve warm.

German Sausage Bake

Makes 8 servings
Hands on: 30 min., Hands off: 55 min.

6 ounces uncooked wide egg noodles
Vegetable cooking spray
1 pound kielbasa sausage, sliced
½ cup chopped onion
2 Granny Smith apples, peeled and
**   coarsely chopped (about 2 cups)**
3 tablespoons butter or margarine
3 tablespoons all-purpose flour
1 (14-ounce) can chicken broth
¼ cup flat beer
1 tablespoon spicy brown mustard
1 teaspoon caraway seeds
½ teaspoon salt
¼ teaspoon pepper
2 cups (8 ounces) shredded Swiss
**   cheese, divided**
1 cup soft, fresh breadcrumbs (such as
**   rye or pumpernickel)**
2 tablespoons butter or margarine,
**   melted**

COOK noodles according to package directions; drain well, and set aside.

COAT a large skillet with cooking spray; add sausage, and cook over medium-high heat until sausage is browned, stirring often. Add onion; cook 2 minutes, stirring often. Stir in apples; remove from heat, and set aside.

MELT 3 tablespoons butter in a heavy saucepan over low heat; add flour, stirring until smooth. Cook, stirring constantly, 1 minute. Gradually add chicken broth and beer; cook over medium heat, stirring constantly until thickened and bubbly. Stir in mustard and next 3 ingredients.

LAYER half of cooked noodles in a greased 13- x 9-inch baking dish. Spoon sausage mixture over noodles; sprinkle 1 cup Swiss cheese evenly over sausage mixture. Top with remaining noodles. Pour chicken broth mixture over noodles. (If desired, cover and chill 8 hours, or freeze up to 1 month; thaw in refrigerator overnight. Let stand at room temperature 30 minutes before baking.)

BAKE, covered, at 350° for 45 minutes or until thoroughly heated. Uncover casserole, and sprinkle with remaining 1 cup Swiss cheese. Combine breadcrumbs and 2 tablespoons melted butter; sprinkle evenly over casserole. Bake 10 more minutes or until cheese melts and breadcrumbs are browned.

Roasted Chicken and Leeks With Sage Biscuit Topping

Makes 6 servings
Hands on: 30 min., Hands off: 35 min.

THE BUTTERY HERBED BISCUIT CRUST ELEVATES THIS DISH BEYOND YOUR ORDINARY CHICKEN POT PIE.

2 cups thinly sliced leeks
2 cups sliced celery
1 tablespoon butter or margarine,
**   melted**
1 (1.8-ounce) package leek soup
**   and recipe mix**
2 cups water
1⅓ cups sour cream
4 cups chopped roasted
**   chicken**
½ cup cold butter or margarine,
**   cut into pieces**
1 cup self-rising flour
2 tablespoons fresh sage
¾ cup milk

COOK sliced leeks and celery in 1 tablespoon melted butter in a large skillet over medium-high heat, stirring constantly until tender; set aside.

COMBINE soup mix and 2 cups water in a saucepan, stirring until smooth; bring to a boil over medium-high heat. Reduce heat; simmer 2 to 4 minutes or until thickened and bubbly. Remove from heat; stir in sour cream.

STIR together leek mixture, soup mixture, and chicken; stir well. Spoon mixture into a lightly greased 11- x 7-inch baking dish. (If desired, cover and chill 8 hours, or freeze up to 1 month; thaw in refrigerator overnight. Remove from refrigerator, and proceed with next step.)

CUT cold butter pieces into flour with pastry blender or fork until mixture is crumbly. Stir in sage. Add milk, stirring just until dry ingredients are moistened. (Mixture will be lumpy.) Spoon batter over casserole mixture.

BAKE, uncovered, at 400° for 35 minutes or until biscuit topping is golden. ▶

Making Chicken Cannelloni

top: To stuff pasta shells, use kitchen scissors to cut each shell lengthwise down one side. **above:** Then spoon stuffing mixture into each shell, and gently press cut sides together.

BEEF LOMBARDI

Makes 6 servings
Hands on: 45 min., Hands off: 40 min.

1 pound lean ground beef
1 (14½-ounce) can chopped tomatoes, undrained
1 (10-ounce) can diced tomatoes and green chiles, undrained
2 teaspoons sugar
2 teaspoons salt
¼ teaspoon pepper
1 (6-ounce) can tomato paste
1 bay leaf
1 (6-ounce) package medium egg noodles
6 green onions, chopped (about ½ cup)
1 cup sour cream
1 cup (4 ounces) shredded sharp Cheddar cheese
1 cup shredded Parmesan cheese
1 cup (4 ounces) shredded mozzarella cheese
Garnish: fresh parsley sprigs

COOK ground beef in a large skillet over medium heat, stirring until it crumbles and is no longer pink. Drain ground beef, and return to skillet.

STIR in chopped tomatoes and next 4 ingredients; cook 5 minutes. Add tomato paste and bay leaf, and simmer 30 minutes. Remove bay leaf.
COOK egg noodles according to package directions; drain.
STIR together cooked egg noodles, chopped green onions, and sour cream until blended.
PLACE noodle mixture in bottom of a lightly greased 13- x 9-inch baking dish. Top with beef mixture; sprinkle evenly with cheeses. (If desired, cover and chill 8 hours, or freeze up to 1 month; thaw in refrigerator overnight. Let stand at room temperature 30 minutes before baking.)
BAKE, covered with aluminum foil, at 350° for 35 minutes. Uncover casserole, and bake 5 more minutes. Garnish, if desired.
TO LIGHTEN: Substitute low-fat or fat-free sour cream and 2% reduced-fat Cheddar cheese. Reduce amount of cheeses on top to ½ cup each.

The combination of three different melted cheeses makes Beef Lombardi irresistible.

CHUNKY HAM POT PIE

Makes 6 to 8 servings
Hands on: 30 min.; Hands off: 1 hr., 5 min.

2 tablespoons butter or margarine
1 cup chopped onion
1 (10-ounce) package frozen cut broccoli or florets
1 pound new potatoes, coarsely chopped
1 (10¾-ounce) can cream of potato soup
1 (8-ounce) carton sour cream
1 cup (4 ounces) shredded sharp Cheddar cheese
¾ cup milk
½ teaspoon garlic powder
½ teaspoon salt
¼ teaspoon pepper
2½ cups chopped cooked ham
½ (15-ounce) package refrigerated piecrusts

MELT 2 tablespoons butter in a large skillet over medium heat; add chopped onion. Cook, stirring often, 10 minutes or until onion is tender and begins to brown. Set aside.

COOK broccoli according to package directions; drain well, and set aside.

COOK chopped new potatoes in boiling water to cover 10 minutes or until barely tender; drain.

COMBINE cream of potato soup and next 6 ingredients in a large bowl, stirring well. Stir in onion, broccoli, new potatoes, and chopped ham. Spoon ham mixture into a lightly greased 3½-quart casserole dish. (Cover and chill 8 hours, if desired. Let stand at room temperature 30 minutes before baking.)

UNROLL piecrust onto a lightly floured surface. Roll pastry to extend ¾ inch beyond edges of casserole. Place pastry over ham mixture. Seal edges, and crimp. Cut slits in pastry to allow steam to escape.

BAKE, uncovered, at 400° for 45 minutes or until crust is golden. Let stand 10 minutes before serving.

NOTE: You can divide this pot pie into 2 (2-quart) dishes. Bake one now, and freeze one for later. You will need the whole package of piecrusts for two casseroles. Top the casserole to be frozen with crust before freezing, but do not cut slits in top until ready to bake. Let frozen casserole stand at room temperature 30 minutes before baking.

BARBECUE BURGER CASSEROLE

Makes 8 servings
Hands on: 30 min., Hands off: 35 min.

THIS IS A GREAT CASSEROLE FOR THE KIDS; ACTUALLY, IT'S PERFECT FOR THE KID IN ALL OF US.

2 pounds ground chuck
1 medium onion, chopped
¾ cup barbecue sauce
¾ cup regular or spicy ketchup
1 tablespoon prepared mustard
1 teaspoon salt
1 teaspoon pepper
1 (8-ounce) package cream cheese, softened
1 (8-ounce) carton sour cream
¾ cup chopped green onions
3 cups hot cooked medium egg noodles
2½ cups (10 ounces) shredded Cheddar or American cheese, divided

Crispy Chicken-and-Rice Casserole is the ideal dish for your neighborhood cooking co-op or potluck dinner. Deliver baked portions with a tossed salad and French bread.

CRISPY CHICKEN-AND-RICE CASSEROLE

Makes 8 to 10 servings
Hands on: 20 min., Hands off: 30 min.

1 cup uncooked long-grain rice
2 cups chopped cooked chicken
2 (10½-ounce) cans cream of mushroom soup
1 (8-ounce) can sliced water chestnuts, drained
1 (3½-ounce) can sliced mushrooms, drained
1 cup chopped celery
¾ cup mayonnaise
1 small onion, chopped
½ cup sliced almonds
1 tablespoon lemon juice
1 teaspoon salt

1 cup crushed cornflakes cereal
Garnish: chopped fresh parsley

COOK rice according to package directions. Stir together cooked rice and next 10 ingredients.

SPOON into a lightly greased 13- x 9-inch baking dish. Sprinkle evenly with cereal.

BAKE at 350° for 30 minutes or until golden and bubbly. Garnish, if desired.

NOTE: Cover and freeze unbaked casserole up to 1 month, if desired. Thaw casserole in refrigerator overnight. Bake, covered with aluminum foil, at 350° for 45 minutes. Remove foil, and bake 15 more minutes or until thoroughly heated.

COOK ground chuck and onion in a large skillet over medium heat until beef crumbles and is no longer pink. Drain and return to skillet.

ADD barbecue sauce and next 4 ingredients to beef mixture. Bring to boil; cover, reduce heat, and simmer, stirring once, 10 minutes.

COMBINE cream cheese and sour cream, stirring until smooth. Stir in green onions and cooked noodles.

LAYER half of noodle mixture in a greased 13- x 9-inch baking dish. Top with half of beef mixture. Sprinkle with 1 cup cheese. Top with remaining noodle mixture and remaining beef mixture. (If desired, cover and chill 8 hours, or freeze up to 1 month; thaw in refrigerator overnight. Let stand at room temperature 30 minutes before baking.)

BAKE, covered, at 350° for 30 minutes or until thoroughly heated. Uncover and sprinkle with remaining 1½ cups cheese; bake 5 more minutes.   ◆

Deli Chicken to the Rescue

Chicken Tetrazzini calls for 3 cups chopped cooked chicken, which is equal to the meat from 1 whole rotisserie chicken.

Stop at the supermarket deli for a fast supper ingredient. Rotisserie chicken is a quick solution for any dish that calls for chopped cooked chicken, and it adds oven-roasted flavor to the recipe. Just remove the meat, chop it up, and refrigerate it up to 3 days for your next meal. Or buy a frozen roasted chicken from the grocer's freezer section, and thaw it in the refrigerator. Mix and match your favorite sides to accompany one of these main dishes.

ZESTY CHICKEN-PASTA SALAD

Makes 4 servings
Hands on: 20 min., Hands off: 1 hr.

ENJOY A QUICK LUNCH WITH THIS MAKE-AHEAD PASTA. TURN TO PAGE 70 FOR MORE MAIN-DISH SALAD RECIPES.

1 (8-ounce) package elbow macaroni
1 (12-ounce) bottle peppercorn-Ranch
  dressing
2½ cups chopped cooked chicken
1 (9-ounce) package frozen sweet
  peas, thawed
1 (2¼-ounce) can sliced black olives,
  drained
1 pint cherry tomatoes, halved
Salt to taste

COOK macaroni according to package directions; drain macaroni, and rinse with cold water.
STIR together macaroni and remaining ingredients in a bowl; cover and chill at least 1 hour.

CHICKEN TETRAZZINI

Makes 6 servings
Hands on: 20 min., Hands off: 25 min.

7 ounces uncooked vermicelli
3 cups chopped cooked chicken
1 cup shredded Parmesan cheese
1 (10¾-ounce) can cream of
  mushroom soup*
1 (10-ounce) container refrigerated
  Alfredo sauce*
1 (3½-ounce) can sliced mushrooms,
  drained
½ cup slivered almonds, toasted
½ cup chicken broth
¼ cup dry sherry
¼ teaspoon freshly ground pepper

CURRIED CHICKEN BISQUE

Makes 6½ cups
Hands on: 20 min., Hands off: 1 hr.

5 cups chicken broth
4 egg yolks
2 cups whipping cream
2 teaspoons curry powder
2 teaspoons lemon pepper seasoning
¼ teaspoon salt
⅛ teaspoon ground red pepper
1 cup finely chopped cooked chicken

BRING chicken broth to a boil in a large heavy saucepan; reduce heat to medium.
WHISK together egg yolks, whipping cream, and next 4 ingredients in a medium bowl; gradually whisk in ½ cup hot chicken broth. Gradually whisk egg yolk mixture into remaining hot broth; cook, whisking constantly, 7 to 10 minutes or until slightly thickened. Cool.
STIR in chopped chicken. Cover and chill at least 1 hour.

COOK pasta according package directions; drain.
STIR together chicken, ½ cup Parmesan cheese, and next 7 ingredients; stir in pasta. Spoon mixture into 6 lightly greased 6-ounce baking dishes or an 11- x 7-inch baking dish. Sprinkle with remaining ½ cup Parmesan cheese.
BAKE at 350° for 25 minutes or until golden and bubbly.
*Reduced-sodium, reduced-fat cream of mushroom soup and light Alfredo sauce may be substituted.

CHICKEN-AND-BRIE QUESADILLAS WITH CHIPOTLE SALSA

Makes 6 to 8 servings
Hands on: 25 min., Hands off: 10 min.

2 cups chopped plum tomatoes
1 small onion, chopped
3 garlic cloves, minced
3 tablespoons fresh lime juice
2 teaspoons minced canned chipotle
  chiles in adobo sauce
½ teaspoon salt
5 green onions, minced and
  divided
½ cup chopped fresh cilantro,
  divided
1 cup finely chopped cooked
  chicken
1 (4.5-ounce) can diced green chiles,
  drained
8 (8-inch) flour tortillas
1 (8-ounce) round Brie, trimmed and
  diced

STIR together first 6 ingredients, ¼ cup green onions, and ¼ cup cilantro. Cover and chill salsa until ready to serve.
STIR together remaining green onions, remaining ¼ cup cilantro, chicken, and diced green chiles.
ARRANGE 4 tortillas on a large lightly greased baking sheet. Top each evenly with diced Brie, chicken mixture, and remaining 4 tortillas, pressing down slightly on each.
BAKE at 425° for 8 to 10 minutes or until cheese melts. Cut each quesadilla into wedges, and serve immediately with chilled salsa.
NOTE: Freeze remaining chipotle chiles in adobo sauce, if desired. ▶

Stuffed Peppers With Chicken and Corn

Makes 8 servings
Hands on: 25 min., Hands off: 35 min.

4 large red bell peppers
1 (12-ounce) package frozen corn soufflé, thawed
3 cups chopped cooked chicken
1 cup fresh corn kernels (about 2 ears)
³/₄ cup soft breadcrumbs
1 (4.5-ounce) can chopped green chiles, drained
¹/₂ medium-size sweet onion, diced
1 tablespoon taco seasoning
2 cups (8 ounces) shredded Monterey Jack cheese with peppers, divided
Garnish: chopped fresh cilantro

CUT peppers in half lengthwise, leaving stems intact; remove seeds. Place cut sides down on a lightly greased baking sheet. Broil 6 inches from heat 4 to 5 minutes or until they begin to blister.
COMBINE corn soufflé and next 6 ingredients; stir in 1 cup cheese.
TURN peppers cut sides up; spoon corn mixture evenly into peppers.
BAKE at 375° for 25 minutes. Top evenly with remaining 1 cup cheese; bake 5 to 10 more minutes or until cheese melts. Garnish, if desired.
NOTE: For testing purposes only, we used Stouffer's Corn Soufflé.

Chicken-Vegetable Pilaf

Makes 6 to 8 servings
Hands on: 25 min., Hands off: 30 min.

¹/₄ cup butter or margarine, divided
1 (8-ounce) package sliced fresh mushrooms
2 celery ribs, sliced
2 cups uncooked long-grain rice
3 (10¹/₂-ounce) cans condensed chicken broth, undiluted
3 cups chopped cooked chicken
1¹/₂ cups shredded carrots (about 3 large carrots)
1 (4-ounce) jar diced pimiento, drained
1 (3.8-ounce) can sliced black olives, drained
¹/₂ teaspoon pepper
¹/₂ cup slivered almonds, toasted

MELT 2 tablespoons butter in a Dutch oven over medium-high heat; add mushrooms and celery, and sauté 4 to 5 minutes or until tender. Remove from pan, and set aside. Wipe pan clean with a paper towel.

MELT remaining 2 tablespoons butter in Dutch oven; add rice, and sauté 6 to 8 minutes or until lightly browned.

STIR in mushroom mixture, broth, and next 5 ingredients; bring to a boil. Cover, reduce heat, and simmer 20 to 25 minutes or until liquid is absorbed. Remove from heat, and let stand 5 minutes.

SPRINKLE with toasted almonds.   ◆

left: The Southwest flavors in Stuffed Peppers With Chicken and Corn get their zest from taco seasoning, Monterey-Jack cheese with peppers, and chopped green chiles. **below:** Creole seasoning gives a spicy kick to Chicken Cakes With Rémoulade Sauce.

CHICKEN CAKES WITH RÉMOULADE SAUCE

Makes 4 servings
Hands on: 30 min.

MAKE SMALLER PATTIES FOR APPETIZER SERVINGS.

2 tablespoons butter or margarine
1/2 red bell pepper, diced
4 green onions, thinly sliced
1 garlic clove, pressed
3 cups chopped cooked chicken
1 cup soft breadcrumbs
1 large egg, lightly beaten
2 tablespoons mayonnaise
1 tablespoon Creole mustard
2 teaspoons Creole seasoning
1/4 cup vegetable oil
Rémoulade Sauce
Garnish: mixed baby greens

MELT butter in a large skillet over medium heat. Add bell pepper, green onions, and garlic, and sauté 3 to 4 minutes or until vegetables are tender.

STIR together bell pepper mixture, chicken, and next 5 ingredients. Shape mixture into 8 (3½-inch) patties.

FRY 4 patties in 2 tablespoons hot oil in a large skillet over medium heat 3 minutes on each side or until golden brown. Drain on paper towels. Repeat procedure with remaining 2 tablespoons oil and patties. Serve immediately with Rémoulade Sauce. Garnish, if desired.

Rémoulade Sauce:

Makes 1¼ cups
Hands on: 5 min.

1 cup mayonnaise
3 green onions, sliced
2 garlic cloves, pressed
2 tablespoons Creole mustard
1 tablespoon chopped fresh parsley
1/4 teaspoon ground red pepper
Garnish: sliced green onions

STIR together first 6 ingredients until well blended. Garnish, if desired.

Italian Flavor

Easy Spaghetti offers savory home-cooked flavor with little fuss.

Luscious sauces, hearty pastas, and seasoned steak make this collection an easy choice for supper. Tuscan Fennel Salad pairs well with any of these recipes. (Or to save time, use bagged lettuce greens from the grocery store to make a simple salad.) For dessert, try Anise Biscuits With Balsamic Strawberries, or flip to page 106 for more sweet selections.

ITALIAN GRILLED STEAK

Makes 4 servings
Hands on: 10 min.; Hands off: 2 hrs., 12 minutes

THIS RECIPE USES THINLY POUNDED STEAKS THAT DON'T REQUIRE A LOT OF TIME ON THE GRILL. SERVE WITH SALAD AND GARLIC BREAD.

4 (1-inch-thick) chuck-eye steaks
1/2 teaspoon salt
1/4 teaspoon pepper
1/2 cup olive oil
1/4 cup balsamic vinegar
2 garlic cloves, chopped
1 teaspoon chopped fresh thyme

PLACE chuck-eye steaks between 2 sheets of heavy-duty plastic wrap; flatten to a 1/2-inch thickness using a meat mallet or rolling pin.
SPRINKLE chuck-eye steaks evenly with salt and pepper.
COMBINE oil and next 3 ingredients in a large shallow dish or heavy-duty zip-top plastic bag; add steaks. Cover or seal; chill 1 to 2 hours.
REMOVE steaks from marinade, discarding marinade.

EASY SPAGHETTI

Makes 4 to 6 servings
Hands on: 20 min., Hands off: 20 min.

PREFER A SPAGHETTI SAUCE THAT HAS SIMMERED ALL DAY? TRY THIS ONE IN A SLOW COOKER. COOK GROUND BEEF AND ONION AS DIRECTED. ADD REMAINING INGREDIENTS EXCEPT SPAGHETTI; SPOON INTO AN ELECTRIC SLOW COOKER. COOK ON LOW 6 TO 7 HOURS OR ON HIGH 3 TO 4 HOURS.

8 to 12 ounces uncooked spaghetti
1 pound ground beef
1 small onion, chopped
2 (14 1/2-ounce) cans Italian-style diced tomatoes, undrained
2 (6-ounce) cans tomato paste
2 teaspoons dried Italian seasoning
1 teaspoon sugar
Garnish: fresh basil sprigs

GRILL steaks, covered with grill lid, over medium-high heat (350° to 400°) 6 minutes on each side or until done.

TUSCAN FENNEL SALAD

Makes 4 to 6 servings
Hands on: 25 min.

FENNEL IS A SWEET ANISE-FLAVORED BULB THAT TASTES GREAT RAW OR COOKED.

2 fennel bulbs
2/3 cup extra virgin olive oil
1/3 cup balsamic vinegar
2 tablespoons sugar
3/4 teaspoon salt
1/2 teaspoon pepper
6 navel oranges, peeled and sectioned
9 medium carrots, sliced
4 celery ribs, chopped
1/2 cup chopped walnuts, toasted
Lettuce leaves

TRIM and discard fennel bases, and trim stalks from bulbs. Cut bulbs lengthwise into fourths; cut into very thin slices.
WHISK together olive oil and next 4 ingredients in a large bowl. Add sliced fennel, orange sections, and next 3 ingredients, tossing gently to coat. Serve over lettuce.

SPINACH-STUFFED SHELLS

Makes 6 servings
Hands on: 20 min., Hands off: 30 min.

18 uncooked jumbo shells
2 (10-ounce) packages frozen chopped spinach, thawed
1 pound lean ground beef
1/4 teaspoon ground nutmeg
1/2 teaspoon salt, divided
1/2 teaspoon pepper, divided
1 (16-ounce) jar marinara sauce
1 (16-ounce) container 1% low-fat cottage cheese
1 large egg
1/4 cup grated Parmesan cheese

COOK pasta shells according to package directions, and drain. Set aside.
DRAIN spinach well, pressing firmly between layers of paper towels. Set aside.
COOK ground beef in a large skillet, stirring until it crumbles and is no longer pink. Drain and pat dry with paper towels. Wipe pan drippings from skillet with a paper towel. Return beef to skillet, and stir in ground nutmeg, 1/4 teaspoon salt, 1/4 teaspoon pepper, and marinara sauce. Set aside.
STIR together spinach, cottage cheese, egg, Parmesan cheese, remaining 1/4 teaspoon salt, and remaining 1/4 teaspoon pepper. Spoon evenly into shells.
SPREAD half of marinara sauce mixture on bottom of a lightly greased 13- x 9-inch baking dish. Arrange stuffed shells over sauce; pour remaining sauce over shells.
BAKE, covered, at 350° for 30 minutes.
NOTE: Stuffed shells and sauce may be frozen up to 1 month before baking. To bake, thaw in refrigerator overnight. Let stand at room temperature 30 minutes. Bake as directed.   ▶

COOK pasta according to package directions; keep warm.
COOK ground beef and onion in a large skillet, stirring until beef crumbles and is no longer pink; drain. Stir in diced tomatoes and next 3 ingredients. Cook, stirring occasionally, over medium heat, about 20 minutes. Serve over hot cooked pasta. Garnish, if desired.

Dried herbs and sautéed onions and garlic embellish canned tomato sauce in Hearty Lasagna.

HEARTY LASAGNA

Makes 9 servings
Hands on: 30 min.; Hands off: 1 hr., 55 min.

LEANER GROUND BEEF AND NONFAT CHEESES LIGHTEN THE FILLING WITHOUT COMPROMISING THE RICHNESS.

12 uncooked lasagna noodles
³⁄₄ pound ground round
1 cup chopped onion
3 garlic cloves, minced
1 (14¹⁄₂-ounce) can diced tomatoes, undrained
1 (14¹⁄₂-ounce) can Italian-style stewed tomatoes, undrained and chopped
1 (8-ounce) can tomato sauce
1 (6-ounce) can tomato paste
1¹⁄₂ tablespoons dried parsley flakes
2 teaspoons dried oregano
1 teaspoon dried basil
¹⁄₄ teaspoon salt
¹⁄₄ teaspoon pepper
2 cups nonfat cottage cheese
¹⁄₂ cup shredded Parmesan cheese
1 (15-ounce) container nonfat ricotta cheese
1 egg white
2 cups (8 ounces) shredded provolone cheese or mozzarella cheese
Garnish: fresh oregano sprigs

COOK noodles according to package directions; drain and set aside.

COOK beef, onion, and garlic in a Dutch oven over medium heat, stirring until beef crumbles and is no longer pink; drain. Wipe pan with a paper towel, and return meat mixture to Dutch oven; add diced tomatoes and next 8 ingredients.

BRING to a boil. Cover, reduce heat, and simmer 15 minutes. Uncover and simmer 20 minutes. Set aside.

COMBINE cottage cheese and next 3 ingredients.

SPREAD ³⁄₄ cup tomato mixture in a lightly greased 13- x 9-inch baking dish. Arrange 4 noodles over tomato mixture; top with half of cottage cheese mixture, 2¹⁄₄ cups tomato mixture, and ²⁄₃ cup shredded cheese. Repeat layers with 4 noodles, remaining cottage cheese mixture, 2¹⁄₄ cups tomato mixture, and ²⁄₃ cup shredded cheese; top with remaining 4 noodles and remaining tomato mixture.

BAKE, covered, at 350° for 1 hour. Uncover and sprinkle with remaining ²⁄₃ cup shredded cheese; bake 10 more minutes or until cheese melts. Let stand 10 minutes before serving. Garnish, if desired.

MARINARA SAUCE

Makes 4 to 6 servings
Hands on: 35 min., Hands off: 40 min.

THIS LIGHT TOMATO SAUCE IS BEST SERVED OVER ANGEL HAIR OR BOW TIE PASTA.

2½ cups chopped onion (about 3 medium)
¼ cup olive oil
3 garlic cloves, pressed
8 large tomatoes, peeled and chopped
2 teaspoons sugar
2 teaspoons dried Italian seasoning
1 teaspoon salt
1 (14½-ounce) can chicken or vegetable broth
¼ cup dry white wine
½ teaspoon anise seeds, crushed (optional)
2 tablespoons chopped fresh parsley

SAUTÉ onion in hot oil in a large heavy saucepan 2 to 3 minutes. Add garlic, and sauté 1 to 2 minutes.

STIR in tomatoes and next 3 ingredients. Gradually add broth, wine, and, if desired, anise seeds.

BRING to a boil; reduce heat, and simmer 35 minutes. Stir in chopped parsley, and simmer 5 minutes.

KITCHEN EXPRESS: Substitute 3 (14.5-ounce) cans diced tomatoes with onion and garlic for first 4 ingredients.

BOLOGNESE SAUCE

Makes about 12 servings
Hands on: 30 min., Hands off: 30 min.

3 tablespoons butter or margarine
1 medium onion, chopped
1 celery rib, chopped
1 carrot, chopped
2 garlic cloves, pressed
¾ pound ground chuck
1 (28-ounce) can crushed tomatoes, undrained
½ cup dry red wine
½ cup beef broth
2 teaspoons dried Italian seasoning
1 teaspoon sugar
½ teaspoon salt
½ teaspoon pepper

MELT butter in a large nonstick skillet over medium-high heat. Add onion and next 3 ingredients; sauté 5 minutes. Add ground chuck; cook, stirring until meat crumbles and is no longer pink; drain.

ADD tomatoes and remaining ingredients; reduce heat to medium, and simmer 30 minutes.

VEGETARIAN BOLOGNESE SAUCE: Substitute 1 medium eggplant, finely chopped, or ¾ pound portobello mushrooms, finely chopped, for ground chuck. Substitute vegetable broth for beef broth. Proceed as directed. ▶

ANISE BISCUITS WITH BALSAMIC STRAWBERRIES

Makes 16 biscuits
Hands on: 20 min., Hands off: 32 min.

YOU CAN ALSO DIP THESE BISCUITS INTO A CUP OF DARK-ROASTED COFFEE.

½ cup butter, softened
¾ cup sugar
3 large eggs
2¼ cups all-purpose flour
1 tablespoon baking powder
⅛ teaspoon salt
¼ cup milk
¾ teaspoon anise extract
Balsamic Strawberries
Garnish: sweetened whipped cream

BEAT butter at medium speed with an electric mixer until creamy; gradually add sugar, beating until blended. Add eggs, 1 at a time, beating well after each addition.

COMBINE flour, baking powder, and salt; add to butter mixture alternately with milk, beginning and ending with flour mixture. Beat at low speed just until blended after each addition. Stir in extract. Spoon batter into a lightly greased 13- x 9-inch pan.

BAKE at 350° for 22 minutes; cool 10 minutes. Cut biscuits with a 2½-inch round or square cutter. Cool completely on wire racks. Split biscuits, and serve with Balsamic Strawberries. Garnish, if desired.

Balsamic Strawberries:

Makes about 2 cups
Hands on: 5 min., Hands off: 1 hr.

1 (16-ounce) container fresh strawberries, sliced
½ cup sugar
3 tablespoons balsamic vinegar

COMBINE all ingredients; let stand 1 hour at room temperature.

Dollop sweetened whipped cream over Anise Biscuits With Balsamic Strawberries.

ALFREDO SAUCE

Makes 6 servings
Hands on: 10 min.

THE HEAT FROM THE COOKED PASTA WILL MELT THE CHEESE IN THIS CREAMY RECIPE.

1 (3-ounce) package refrigerated finely shredded Parmesan cheese
½ cup butter or margarine, melted
½ cup whipping cream
2 tablespoons chopped fresh parsley
¼ teaspoon ground white pepper
Hot cooked linguine

COMBINE first 5 ingredients in a bowl; toss with hot cooked pasta.

Alfredo Sauce tossed with your favorite hot cooked pasta is a great side dish for almost any meal.

Lasagna

principles of pasta

Pasta comes in all shapes and sizes. When choosing one, consider the size of the other ingredients in the dish. Review our chart below for uses of various types.

Cook pasta until al dente—pliable but firm to the bite. Cooking times vary with pasta size, shape, and moisture content. Fresh pasta cooks in 1 to 3 minutes, while dried pasta can require up to 20 minutes. If pasta sticks together, add 1 to 2 tablespoons oil to the cooking water.

Lasagna
This wide, flat noodle can have smooth or ruffled edges. It is usually layered or rolled in dishes with cheese or meat sauces. Try Hearty Lasagna on page 46.

Shells
Shells come in small, medium, and jumbo sizes. Use small ones with thinner sauces that can get inside the shells and jumbo ones for stuffing with cheese or meat mixtures. Try Spinach-Stuffed Shells on page 45.

Orzo
When you need a pasta that cooks fast (about 5 minutes), choose orzo. Toss it with butter and Parmesan cheese as a substitute for rice or potatoes. Enjoy orzo mixed with bottled Parmesan dressing and assorted fresh vegetables for a light salad.

Penne
Penne is a sturdy tube shape that goes best with thick or chunky sauces. Try it with Bolognese Sauce on page 47.

Manicotti
This tubelike pasta is best stuffed with cheese or meat mixtures. It is first boiled and then stuffed and covered with a sauce before being baked.

Fettuccine and Linguine
These have more surface area for sauces to cling to; they complement cream, butter, or seafood sauces. Fettuccine (top) is wider than linguine.

Bow Ties
Specialty products such as bow ties (farfalle), alphabet shapes, and wagon wheels can be substituted cup for cup for those pastas of similar shape and size. For example, substitute small wagon wheels for small shells. ◆

Shells

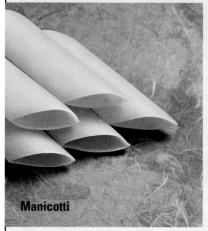
Orzo

Penne

Manicotti

Fettuccine and Linguine

Bow Ties

in the **mood** for...

To enjoy the flavors of the Far East, sample these recipes. Spinach Egg Drop Soup makes an easy appetizer. Then choose from a variety of entrées such as Sesame-Crusted Turkey Mignons. Round out your meal with Asian Slaw, or try Baby Spinach With Pine Nuts for a quick skillet side.

Asian Flair

A mixture of sesame seeds, fresh ginger, flavored oil, and other seasonings coats Sesame-Crusted Turkey Mignons.

SESAME-CRUSTED TURKEY MIGNONS

Makes 4 servings
Hands on: 20 min., Hands off: 24 min.

1/2 cup sesame seeds, toasted
1/4 cup olive oil
1 garlic clove, minced
1 tablespoon chopped fresh chives
1 tablespoon soy sauce
2 teaspoons fresh lemon juice
1 teaspoon grated fresh ginger
1/2 teaspoon dark sesame oil
2 (11-ounce) packages turkey mignons*
Garnishes: halved lemon slices, chopped fresh parsley or cilantro
Creamy Wine Sauce (optional)
Hot cooked noodles (optional)

STIR together first 8 ingredients; dredge turkey in sesame seed mixture. Place on a greased rack in a broiler pan.
BROIL 5½ inches from heat 12 minutes on each side or until done. Place turkey on a platter; garnish, if desired. Serve with Creamy Wine Sauce and hot cooked noodles, if desired.
*2 turkey tenderloins, cut in half, may be substituted for turkey mignons.

Creamy Wine Sauce:
Makes ¾ cup
Hands on: 20 min.
THIS SAUCE IS DELICIOUS SERVED WITH SESAME-CRUSTED TURKEY MIGNONS OR JUST OVER PASTA.

1 cup fruity white wine*
2 teaspoons lemon juice
1/4 cup whipping cream
1/3 cup butter or margarine
2 tablespoons soy sauce

BRING wine and lemon juice to a boil over medium-high heat. Boil 6 to 8 minutes or until mixture is reduced by half. Whisk in cream. Cook 3 to 4 minutes, whisking constantly, until thickened.
REDUCE heat to a simmer; whisk in butter and soy sauce until butter is melted.
*1 cup white grape juice may be substituted for fruity white wine.
NOTE: For testing purposes only, we used Liebfraumilch for wine.

Spinach Egg Drop Soup

Makes 6 cups
Hands on: 30 min.

FOR EXTRA TEXTURE, FLAVOR, AND COLOR, ADD SLICED FRESH SHIITAKE OR BUTTON MUSHROOMS AND THINLY SLICED RED BELL PEPPER. SPRINKLE SLICES INTO EMPTY BOWLS, AND THEN LADLE THE SOUP OVER THE VEGETABLES.

**6 cups fat-free reduced-sodium
   chicken broth
1 large egg, lightly beaten
1 tablespoon soy sauce
$\frac{1}{2}$ teaspoon sugar
2 green onions, chopped
2 cups fresh spinach**

BRING broth to a boil; reduce heat to a simmer. Slowly add egg, stirring constantly, until egg forms lacy strands. Immediately remove from heat. Let stand 1 minute. Stir in soy sauce, sugar, and green onions. Divide spinach evenly between 6 bowls; ladle soup over spinach. Serve immediately.

Fluffy White Rice

Makes 4 servings
Hands on: 5 min., Hands off: 25 min.

RINSING THE RICE BEFORE COOKING REDUCES ITS STARCHINESS, MAKING FOR A FLUFFY, NOT STICKY, PRODUCT.

**1 cup uncooked long-grain rice
1$\frac{1}{2}$ cups water
1 teaspoon vegetable oil**

PLACE rice in a large bowl. Rinse with water 3 or 4 times or until water is no longer cloudy; drain.
BRING rice, 1½ cups water, and oil to a boil in a heavy saucepan. Cover, reduce heat, and simmer 15 minutes or until rice is tender. Remove from heat, and let stand 10 minutes. Fluff with a fork.

Peanutty Beef Stir-fry

Makes 4 servings
Hands on: 30 min.

**8 ounces linguine
1$\frac{1}{4}$ pounds lean boneless
   top sirloin steak
3 tablespoons lite soy sauce
2 to 3 tablespoons brown sugar
3 tablespoons creamy peanut butter
2 teaspoons lemon juice
$\frac{1}{2}$ teaspoon garlic powder
$\frac{1}{8}$ to $\frac{1}{4}$ teaspoon crushed red pepper
$\frac{1}{4}$ teaspoon ground black pepper
2 teaspoons sesame or vegetable oil**

Add dried crushed red pepper for a little more heat in Beef With Ginger.

Beef With Ginger

Makes 4 servings
Hands on: 30 min.

CHILLING THE BEEF IN THE FREEZER FOR 5 MINUTES MAKES IT EASIER TO CUT INTO VERY THIN SLICES.

**Fluffy White Rice (see recipe)
1 pound sirloin steak, chilled
$\frac{1}{2}$ teaspoon pepper
$\frac{1}{4}$ teaspoon salt
$\frac{1}{2}$ cup fat-free reduced-sodium
   beef broth
2 teaspoons cornstarch
2 tablespoons grated fresh ginger
2 teaspoons vegetable oil
$\frac{1}{2}$ teaspoon minced garlic
2 teaspoons lite soy sauce
6 green onions, cut diagonally
   into 1-inch pieces
$\frac{1}{2}$ teaspoon dried crushed red pepper
   (optional)
Garnish: green onion curls**

PREPARE Fluffy White Rice as directed; keep warm.

CUT chilled steak diagonally across the grain into very thin slices. Sprinkle with pepper and salt; set aside.
STIR together beef broth and cornstarch in a small bowl until smooth; set cornstarch mixture aside.
SAUTÉ ginger in hot oil in a large nonstick skillet over high heat 2 minutes or until tan-colored. Add garlic, and sauté 30 seconds. Add steak; cook 2 minutes, stirring constantly. Stir in soy sauce.
STIR cornstarch mixture, and drizzle over beef mixture in skillet. Cook, stirring constantly, 1 minute or until thickened. Add green onions, and, if desired, crushed red pepper; cook 1 minute. Serve immediately over Fluffy White Rice; garnish, if desired.

**1 red bell pepper, cut into
   1-inch pieces
4 green onions, cut into 1-inch pieces**
COOK pasta according to package directions; drain and keep warm.
TRIM fat from steak; slice steak diagonally across grain into $\frac{1}{8}$-inch-wide strips. Set aside.
WHISK together soy sauce, brown sugar, and next 5 ingredients until smooth.
HEAT oil in a large nonstick skillet over medium-high heat 1 minute. Add steak; stir-fry 2 minutes. Add bell pepper and green onions; stir-fry 2 minutes or until steak is no longer pink. Stir in soy sauce mixture; cover and cook 3 minutes or until thoroughly heated. Toss with hot cooked pasta. ▶

CHICKEN-AND-SNOW PEA STIR-FRY

Makes 4 servings
Hands on: 35 min.

Fluffy White Rice (see recipe)
¾ cup chicken broth
¼ cup soy sauce
1½ tablespoons cornstarch
2 skinned and boned chicken breasts, cut into ¼-inch-wide strips
1 tablespoon peanut or vegetable oil
4 celery ribs, sliced
¼ pound fresh snow peas, trimmed
4 large mushrooms, sliced
3 green onions, sliced
1 (2-ounce) package slivered almonds, toasted
Garnish: green onion strips

PREPARE Fluffy White Rice as directed, and keep warm.

STIR together broth, soy sauce, and cornstarch.

COOK chicken in hot oil in a large skillet over medium-high heat, stirring constantly, 6 minutes or until almost done. Add celery and next 3 ingredients, and cook, stirring constantly, 3 to 4 minutes or until vegetables are crisp-tender and chicken is done. Stir in broth mixture. Bring to a boil, stirring constantly; boil, stirring constantly, 1 minute. Serve over Fluffy White Rice, and sprinkle with almonds. Garnish, if desired.

Peanut oil—with good monounsaturated fat—is a heart-healthy choice for cooking Chicken-and-Snow Pea Stir-fry.

Thread bell peppers, baby corn, or any of your favorite vegetables onto skewers for Asian Chicken Kabobs.

ASIAN CHICKEN KABOBS

Makes 4 servings
Hands on: 30 min.

1½ pounds skinned and boned chicken breasts, cut into 1-inch pieces
¼ teaspoon salt
¼ teaspoon pepper
1 yellow bell pepper, cut into 1-inch pieces
1 red bell pepper, cut into 1-inch pieces
1 (15-ounce) can whole baby corn, drained and cut in half
4 metal or wooden skewers
⅓ cup hoisin or teriyaki sauce
⅓ cup honey
1 garlic clove, pressed
½ teaspoon minced fresh ginger
Hot cooked rice (optional)

SPRINKLE chicken evenly with salt and pepper.
THREAD chicken, bell pepper pieces, and corn alternately onto skewers.
COMBINE hoisin sauce and next 3 ingredients; brush on kabobs.
GRILL kabobs, covered with grill lid, over medium-high heat (350° to 400°) 12 minutes, turning and basting often with hoisin sauce mixture. Serve with hot cooked rice, if desired.
NOTE: If using wooden skewers, soak in water 30 minutes before using to prevent burning.

BABY SPINACH WITH PINE NUTS

Makes 4 servings
Hands on: 10 min.

SESAME OIL ACCENTS THIS EASY SAUTÉ WITH SUBTLE NUTTY FLAVOR. USE OLIVE OIL IF YOU DON'T HAVE SESAME OIL.

2 (7-ounce) packages fresh baby spinach
2 garlic cloves, minced
1 teaspoon sesame or olive oil
¼ teaspoon salt
¼ teaspoon pepper
2 tablespoons pine nuts, toasted*

SAUTÉ spinach and garlic in hot oil in a large nonstick skillet over medium-high heat 5 minutes or until spinach wilts. Stir in salt and pepper; sprinkle with pine nuts. Serve immediately.
*2 tablespoons chopped toasted pecans or sliced toasted almonds may be substituted for pine nuts.

ASIAN SLAW

Makes 8 to 10 servings
Hands on: 15 min., Hands off: 24 hrs.

2 (3-ounce) packages beef-flavored ramen noodle soup mix
2 (8.5-ounce) packages coleslaw mix
1 cup sliced almonds, toasted
1 cup sunflower kernels
1 bunch green onions, chopped
½ cup sugar
¾ cup vegetable oil
⅓ cup white vinegar

REMOVE flavor packets from soup mix, and reserve for later use; crush noodles. Place noodles in bottom of a large bowl. Top with slaw mix; sprinkle with toasted almonds, sunflower kernels, and chopped green onions.
WHISK together contents from flavor packets, sugar, oil, and vinegar; pour over slaw. Cover and chill 24 hours. Toss before serving. ◆

Tasty Tex-Mex

Bean-and-Vegetable Soft Tacos
are ready in 25 minutes.

Spice up your meal by mixing and matching any of these Southwestern selections. Serve Texas Grilled Sirloin and Serrano Chile Salsa next to Rice With Black Beans and Corn, or pair Tortilla-Corn Chowder and Mexican Cornsticks. With a list of options this long, you won't run out of supper ideas.

BURRITO CASSEROLE

Makes 6 to 8 servings
Hands on: 20 min., Hands off: 40 min.

WARMING FLOUR TORTILLAS IN THE MICROWAVE OR OVEN MAKES THEM MORE PLIABLE AND EASIER TO ROLL UP.

1½ cups tomato juice
1 (1¼-ounce) envelope taco seasoning
   mix
½ pound ground beef
1 (16-ounce) can refried beans
3 cups (12 ounces) shredded Cheddar
   cheese, divided
8 (8-inch) flour tortillas, warmed
1 small avocado, peeled and cubed
1 tablespoon lemon juice
1½ cups shredded lettuce
1 tomato, chopped

COMBINE tomato juice and taco seasoning mix.
COOK ground beef in a large skillet, stir-ring until it crumbles and is no longer pink; drain and return to skillet. Stir in refried beans and ½ cup tomato juice mixture. Bring to a boil; cover, reduce heat, and simmer, stirring occasionally, 5 minutes or until beef mixture is thoroughly heated. Remove from heat.
PLACE ¼ cup beef mixture and 2½ tablespoons cheese evenly down center of each tortilla. Roll up tortillas, and place, seam sides down, in a lightly greased 13- x 9-inch baking dish.
POUR remaining 1 cup tomato juice mixture over casserole.
BAKE, covered, at 350° for 30 to 35 minutes. Uncover and sprinkle with remaining cheese; bake 5 more minutes or until cheese melts.
COMBINE avocado and lemon juice. Sprinkle avocado, lettuce, and tomato over casserole. Serve immediately.

BEAN-AND-VEGETABLE SOFT TACOS

Makes 6 tacos
Hands on: 25 min.

3 tablespoons red wine vinegar
1 teaspoon vegetable oil
½ teaspoon ground cumin
¼ teaspoon salt
⅛ teaspoon black pepper
1 cup shredded zucchini (about 1
   zucchini)
1 cup shredded yellow squash (about
   1 squash)
½ red bell pepper, chopped
1 small onion, chopped
1 (16-ounce) can black beans, rinsed
   and drained
¼ cup water
½ teaspoon chili powder
¼ teaspoon salt
¼ teaspoon garlic powder
¼ teaspoon dried crushed red pepper
6 (6-inch) flour tortillas, warmed

1 cup (4 ounces) shredded Monterey
   Jack cheese with peppers
Garnish: fresh cilantro sprigs

WHISK together first 5 ingredients in a large bowl. Add zucchini and next 3 ingredients; toss gently. Set aside.
COMBINE black beans and next 5 ingredients in a saucepan. Bring to a boil; reduce heat, and simmer 3 to 5 minutes or until thoroughly heated.
SPOON zucchini mixture evenly down center of each tortilla. Top evenly with bean mixture and cheese. Roll up tortillas; secure each with a wooden pick. Garnish, if desired.
KITCHEN EXPRESS: Omit vinegar, oil, ¼ teaspoon salt, and black pepper; stir ½ teaspoon ground cumin into ½ cup Italian dressing. Proceed as directed.

CHICKEN ENCHILADAS

Makes 6 to 8 servings
Hands on: 15 min., Hands off: 25 min.

2 cups chopped cooked chicken
1 (16-ounce) container cottage
   cheese
1 (8-ounce) container sour cream
4 green onions, chopped
¼ teaspoon salt
8 (8-inch) flour tortillas, warmed
1 cup (4 ounces) shredded Monterey
   Jack cheese with peppers
1 (10-ounce) can enchilada sauce
Toppings: shredded Cheddar cheese,
   sour cream, sliced black olives

COMBINE chicken and next 4 ingredients; spoon about ⅓ cup of chicken mixture down center of each tortilla, and sprinkle evenly with Monterey Jack cheese. Roll up tortillas, and place, seam sides down, in a lightly greased 13- x 9-inch baking dish. Pour enchilada sauce evenly over tortillas.
BAKE, covered, at 350° for 25 minutes. Serve with desired toppings.
SPINACH ENCHILADAS: Substitute 1 (10-ounce) package frozen chopped spinach, thawed and well drained, for chopped cooked chicken. Proceed with recipe as directed.

PICO DE GALLO

Makes ¾ cup
Hands on: 10 min., Hands off: 8 hrs.

SERVE WITH TORTILLA CHIPS OR ON TACOS.

2 medium tomatoes, seeded and
   chopped
½ small onion, chopped
1 jalapeño, seeded and minced
3 tablespoons chopped fresh
   cilantro
2 tablespoons lime juice
⅛ teaspoon salt

COMBINE all ingredients. Cover and chill 8 hours.   ▶

Tortilla-Corn Chowder is an easy way to satisfy your craving for Tex-Mex.

CHILES RELLENOS

Makes 4 servings
Hands on: 20 min., Hands off: 10 min.

8 fresh Anaheim or poblano chile
   peppers
1 (8-ounce) block longhorn or
   Monterey Jack cheese
1 large egg
¹/₃ cup milk
³/₄ cup all-purpose flour
³/₄ cup yellow cornmeal
1 teaspoon salt
Vegetable oil
Serrano Chile Salsa (see recipe on
   page 59)

BROIL peppers on an aluminum foil-lined baking sheet 5 inches from heat about 5 minutes on each side or until peppers look blistered. Place peppers in a zip-top plastic freezer bag; seal and let stand 10 minutes to loosen skins. Peel peppers.

CUT a small slit in 1 side of each pepper, forming a pocket. Cut cheese into 8 strips; place cheese strips inside chiles, and secure with wooden picks.

COMBINE egg and milk in a small bowl. Combine flour, cornmeal, and salt in an-other bowl. Dredge chiles in flour mixture; dip in egg mixture, and dredge in flour mixture again.

POUR oil to a depth of 2 inches in a skillet; heat to 375°. Fry chiles, 2 at a time, 1 minute on each side or until golden. Drain on paper towels. Serve immediately with Serrano Chile Salsa.

MEXICAN CORNSTICKS

Makes 16 cornsticks
Hands on: 10 min., Hands off: 20 min.

1¹/₄ cups all-purpose flour
³/₄ cup yellow cornmeal*
2 teaspoons baking powder
1 teaspoon baking soda
¹/₂ teaspoon salt
¹/₈ teaspoon ground red pepper
³/₄ cup buttermilk
1 (8³/₄-ounce) can cream-style corn
1 (4.5-ounce) can chopped green
   chiles, undrained
1 large egg
¹/₂ cup (2 ounces) shredded sharp
   Cheddar cheese

COMBINE first 6 ingredients in a medium bowl; make a well in center of mixture.

COMBINE buttermilk and next 4 ingredients; add to center of dry ingredients, stirring until moistened. Spoon into lightly greased cast-iron or traditional cornstick pans, filling two-thirds full.

BAKE at 425° for 18 to 20 minutes or until golden. Remove from pans immediately.
*Yellow cornmeal mix may be substituted for cornmeal. Omit baking powder and baking soda; proceed as directed.

CHILE CORNBREAD SALAD

Makes 8 to 10 servings
Hands on: 30 min., Hands off: 2 hrs.

1 (6-ounce) package Mexican
   cornbread mix
1 (4.5-ounce) can chopped green
   chiles
1 (1-ounce) package Ranch dressing
   mix
1 (8-ounce) container light sour
   cream
1 cup light mayonnaise
2 (16-ounce) cans pinto beans, rinsed
   and drained
1 green bell pepper, chopped
2 (15¹/₄-ounce) cans whole kernel
   corn, drained
3 large tomatoes, chopped
10 bacon slices, cooked and
   crumbled
2 cups (8 ounces) shredded reduced-
   fat Cheddar cheese
1 cup sliced green onions
Lettuce leaves

PREPARE cornbread mix according to package directions, adding chopped green chiles; cool.

COMBINE dressing mix, sour cream, and mayonnaise.

CRUMBLE half of cornbread into a bowl. Top with half each of pinto beans, sour cream mixture, chopped bell pepper, and next 5 ingredients. Repeat layers, starting with cornbread and ending with green onions.

COVER and chill 2 hours. Serve salad in lettuce-lined bowls. ▶

TORTILLA-CORN CHOWDER

Makes 2 quarts
Hands on: 20 min.; Hands off: 1 hr., 15 min.

6 large ears fresh corn
3 (14-ounce) cans chicken broth
1 large onion, chopped
2 garlic cloves, pressed
4 (6-inch) corn tortillas, coarsely
   chopped
1 (4.5-ounce) can chopped green
   chiles, undrained
¹/₂ cup sour cream
2 to 3 tablespoons chopped fresh
   cilantro
¹/₄ teaspoon salt
¹/₄ teaspoon pepper
Garnishes: crushed tortilla chips,
   sour cream, fresh cilantro sprigs

CUT corn kernels from cob into a Dutch oven; scrape milk and remaining pulp from cobs into Dutch oven. Add broth and next 3 ingredients. Bring to a boil; cover, reduce heat, and simmer, stirring occasionally, 1 hour and 15 minutes.

STIR in green chiles and next 4 ingredients. Cook until thoroughly heated. Garnish, if desired.

tortilla soup two ways

below: Chopped tortillas are added to the corn mixture of Tortilla-Corn Chowder, giving the soup its delicious thickness.

below: For a creamier Tortilla-Corn Chowder, puree cooked corn-tortilla mixture; then add chopped green chiles and remaining ingredients.

For this deliciously different version of Plum Good Fajitas, substitute grilled chicken for steak.

Serve Plum Good Fajitas with Pico de Gallo or your favorite salsa.

PLUM GOOD FAJITAS

Makes 8 servings
Hands on: 45 min.

LOOK FOR PLUM SAUCE IN THE ETHNIC FOODS AISLE.

1 tablespoon butter
1 small onion, chopped
1 (7.6-ounce) jar Asian plum sauce
½ (6-ounce) can frozen lemonade concentrate, thawed and undiluted
½ cup chili sauce
¼ cup soy sauce
1 tablespoon dry mustard
1 teaspoon ground ginger
1 teaspoon Worcestershire sauce
¼ teaspoon hot sauce
1 red bell pepper, cut into strips
1 green bell pepper, cut into strips
1 large red onion, sliced
2 (1-pound) flank steaks*
8 (8-inch) flour tortillas, warmed
Toppings: chopped red onions, Pico de Gallo (see recipe on page 55), guacamole

MELT butter in a medium saucepan over medium-high heat; add chopped onion, and sauté until tender. Stir in plum sauce and next 7 ingredients. Bring sauce to a boil; reduce heat, and simmer 15 minutes.

SAUTÉ bell peppers and onion slices in a large skillet over medium-high heat until crisp-tender. Keep warm.

GRILL flank steaks, without grill lid, over high heat (400° to 500°) 20 minutes or to desired degree of doneness, basting often with plum sauce mixture and turning steaks once.

CUT diagonally across the grain into thin strips. Serve steak and vegetables with tortillas and desired toppings.

*2 pounds skinned and boned chicken breasts may be substituted. Grill over medium-high heat (350° to 400°) 7 minutes on each side or until done, basting often. Cut chicken into thin strips.

SKILLET FAJITAS: Omit grilling procedure. Cut steak or chicken into thin strips. Cook strips, in batches, in 1 tablespoon hot olive oil in a large skillet over medium-high heat, stirring often, 10 minutes or until done. Stir in ¼ cup plum sauce mixture; cook until thoroughly heated. Serve steak or chicken strips with remaining plum sauce mixture, tortillas, and desired toppings.

TEXAS GRILLED SIRLOIN AND SERRANO CHILE SALSA

Makes 4 servings
Hands on: 15 min.; Hands off: 1 hr., 16 min.

1 pound lean boneless top sirloin steak, trimmed
¼ cup lime juice
2 tablespoons chopped fresh or 2 teaspoons dried oregano
1 tablespoon chopped fresh or 2 teaspoons dried cilantro
1 teaspoon pepper
1 garlic clove, pressed
½ teaspoon salt
Serrano Chile Salsa
Garnishes: fresh cilantro sprigs, lime slices

COMBINE steak and next 5 ingredients in a large zip-top plastic freezer bag; seal and shake well. Chill 1 hour, turning occasionally.

REMOVE steak from marinade, discarding marinade. Sprinkle steak evenly with salt. Grill steak, covered with grill lid, over medium-high heat (350° to 400°) 7 to 8 minutes on each side or to desired degree of doneness. Cut diagonally across the grain into thin slices. Serve with Serrano Chile Salsa. Garnish, if desired.

Serrano Chile Salsa:

Makes 2 cups
Hands on: 15 min., Hands off: 1 hr.

6 serrano chile peppers, diced
1 pound plum tomatoes, diced
¼ cup orange juice
2 tablespoons diced red onion
2 tablespoons diced yellow or red bell pepper
2 tablespoons minced fresh cilantro
1 tablespoon rice vinegar
½ teaspoon salt
½ teaspoon sugar

COMBINE serrano chile peppers and remaining ingredients; cover and chill 1 hour.

▶

Edible shells hold Chicken-Black Bean Salad.

CHICKEN-BLACK BEAN SALAD

Makes 6 servings
Hands on: 30 min.

FOR A MILDER DEGREE OF HEAT, REMOVE THE SEEDS FROM THE JALAPEÑO PEPPERS BEFORE CHOPPING.

3 tablespoons olive oil
1 tablespoon lemon juice
3 garlic cloves, minced
2 jalapeño peppers, chopped
2 tablespoons chopped fresh
    oregano
1½ teaspoons ground cumin
½ teaspoon salt
½ teaspoon pepper
3 cups chopped cooked chicken
1 (15-ounce) can black beans,
    rinsed and drained
1 cup frozen whole kernel corn,
    thawed
1 large tomato, diced
3 tablespoons chopped fresh
    cilantro
6 taco salad shells
6 to 8 cups shredded lettuce
Garnish: fresh cilantro sprigs

WHISK together first 8 ingredients in a large bowl. Add chicken and next 4 ingredients, tossing to coat. Cover and chill, if desired.

HEAT taco shells according to package directions. Fill shells with shredded lettuce; top evenly with chicken mixture. Garnish, if desired.

FLAUTAS

Makes 6 to 8 servings
Hands on: 15 min., Hands off: 5 hrs.

2 (2½-pound) beef briskets, trimmed
1 medium onion, peeled and quartered
1 garlic bulb, peeled
2 teaspoons salt
⅔ cup sour cream
¼ cup whipping cream
20 (8-inch) flour tortillas, warmed
1 cup vegetable oil
Toppings: shredded lettuce, shredded
    Monterey Jack cheese, chopped
    tomato, salsa

PLACE beef briskets in a Dutch oven, and add water to cover. Add onion quarters, garlic bulb, and salt; bring to a boil. Cover, reduce heat, and simmer 4 to 5 hours or until tender, adding more water to Dutch oven as needed.

REMOVE brisket from Dutch oven, discarding vegetables; chill. Shred brisket with a fork; set aside.

COMBINE sour cream and whipping cream; cover and chill mixture until ready to serve.

SPOON ½ cup shredded brisket down center of each tortilla; roll up tortillas, and place, seam sides down, in a 13- x 9-inch baking dish. Cover and keep warm.

REMOVE filled tortillas from baking dish, and cook, seam sides down, in hot oil in a large skillet over medium-high heat until golden brown on both sides. Drain on paper towels. Serve flautas warm with sour cream mixture and desired toppings.

TOSTADAS

Makes 6 servings
Hands on: 20 min.

1½ pounds lean ground beef
1 small onion, chopped
1 garlic clove, pressed
½ teaspoon salt
2 teaspoons chili powder
Vegetable oil
6 (8-inch) flour tortillas
1 (15-ounce) can kidney beans, rinsed
    and drained
1 large tomato, chopped
½ pound iceberg lettuce, shredded
1 large avocado, peeled and chopped
2 cups (8 ounces) shredded sharp
    Cheddar cheese
Toppings: sour cream, salsa

COOK first 5 ingredients in a large skillet over medium heat, stirring until beef crumbles and is no longer pink; drain and set aside.

POUR oil to a depth of ¼ inch into a heavy skillet. Fry tortillas, 1 at a time, in hot oil over high heat 20 seconds on each side or until crisp and golden brown. Drain on paper towels.

LAYER beef mixture, beans, tomato, and next 3 ingredients on warm tortillas. Serve with desired toppings.

Beef-and-Bean Chimichangas

Makes 8 to 10 servings
Hands on: 30 min.

1 pound ground chuck
1 medium onion, chopped
2 garlic cloves, pressed
$\frac{1}{4}$ teaspoon salt
1 (16-ounce) can refried beans
$\frac{1}{2}$ cup tomato sauce
1 tablespoon chili powder
$\frac{3}{4}$ teaspoon ground cumin
10 (10-inch) flour tortillas, warmed
Vegetable oil
Salsa Verde
2 cups (8 ounces) shredded Monterey
   Jack cheese

COOK first 4 ingredients in a large skillet until meat is browned, stirring until it crumbles. Drain; stir in refried beans and next 3 ingredients.

PLACE $\frac{1}{3}$ cup meat mixture just below center of each tortilla.

FOLD bottom edge of tortilla over meat filling; fold in left and right sides. Roll up to form a rectangle, and secure with a wooden pick.

POUR oil to a depth of 2 inches into a Dutch oven, and heat to 375°. Fry chimichangas, in batches, $1\frac{1}{2}$ minutes on each side or until golden brown. Drain on paper towels. Remove wooden picks.

ARRANGE chimichangas on a large ovenproof platter or baking sheet; top with Salsa Verde, and sprinkle evenly with Monterey Jack cheese.

BROIL $5\frac{1}{2}$ inches from heat 1 to 2 minutes or until cheese melts. Serve immediately.

Salsa Verde:
Makes 2 cups
Hands on: 15 min.

5 Anaheim chile peppers, seeded
1 large jalapeño pepper, seeded
1 large onion, diced
1 small tomato, diced
2 garlic cloves, minced
$\frac{1}{4}$ cup fresh cilantro leaves
$\frac{1}{4}$ cup lime juice
$\frac{1}{4}$ teaspoon salt
$\frac{1}{4}$ teaspoon sugar
$\frac{1}{4}$ teaspoon ground cumin

COMBINE all ingredients in a bowl; cover and chill until ready to serve.   ◆

Rice With Black Beans And Corn

Makes 8 servings
Hands on: 20 min., Hands off: 20 min.

WHILE THE RICE SIMMERS, PREP THE REST OF THE INGREDIENTS FOR THIS QUICK SIDE.

1 cup water
$\frac{1}{2}$ cup uncooked long-grain rice
4 plum tomatoes, chopped
1 (15-ounce) can black beans,
   rinsed and drained
1 (10-ounce) package frozen whole
   kernel corn, thawed
4 green onions, chopped
$\frac{1}{2}$ cup chopped fresh cilantro
$\frac{1}{4}$ cup lime juice
1 teaspoon salt
$\frac{1}{4}$ teaspoon pepper

BRING 1 cup water to a boil in a large saucepan; stir in rice. Cover, reduce heat, and simmer 20 minutes or until liquid is absorbed and rice is tender.

ADD tomatoes and remaining ingredients. Cook over medium heat, stirring constantly until heated.

Rice With Black Beans and Corn is the perfect side for a hungry crowd.

Fish and Seafood

Fried Catfish with Buttermilk Hush Puppies, Creamy Sweet Slaw, and baked beans is the ultimate outdoor feast.

You might typically reserve fish and seafood for weekends, but these recipes will help you discover what speedy and healthful additions they are to weeknight meals. Shrimp require sautéing just until they turn pink (about 4 to 5 minutes), and fish fillets only need to cook until they easily flake with a fork (about 4 to 6 minutes on each side). Try our serving suggestions with any one of these tasty, time-saving choices.

FRIED CATFISH

Makes 8 servings
Hands on: 30 min.
5 large eggs
1 cup milk
1 teaspoon salt
$^1/_4$ teaspoon pepper
1 (16-ounce) package saltines
8 catfish fillets ($3^1/_2$ to 4 pounds)
Vegetable oil

WHISK together first 4 ingredients.
PROCESS saltine crackers, in batches, in a food processor until finely crushed. Dip fish in egg mixture; dredge in cracker crumbs.
POUR oil to a depth of 5 inches in a Dutch oven; heat to 375°. Fry fish, in batches, 4 to 6 minutes on each side or until fish flakes with a fork. Drain on paper towels.

BUTTERMILK HUSH PUPPIES

Makes 5 dozen
Hands on: 30 min.
2 cups self-rising flour
2 cups self-rising white cornmeal
1 teaspoon sugar
$^1/_2$ teaspoon salt
$^1/_2$ teaspoon pepper
1 large onion, grated
1 jalapeño pepper, seeded and minced (optional)
2 cups buttermilk
1 large egg
Vegetable oil

COMBINE first 5 ingredients; stir in onion and, if desired, jalapeño.
WHISK together buttermilk and egg; add to flour mixture.
POUR oil to a depth of 3 inches in a Dutch oven; heat to 375°. Drop batter by level tablespoonfuls into oil; fry, in batches, 5 to 7 minutes or until golden. Drain on paper towels.

---

make a menu

shrimp, scallops, or seafood pasta
Greek Tomatoes (page 99)
or tossed salad
Lemon-Raspberry
Parfaits (page 106)

grilled fish
Lemon Couscous (page 103)
Herbed Vegetable
Medley (page 101)
Watermelon Sorbet (page 106)

Southern fried catfish
baked beans
Creamy Sweet Slaw (page 99)
Buttermilk Hush Puppies
Very Berry Cobbler (page 107)

TUNA WITH SAUTÉED VEGETABLES

Makes 4 servings
Hands on: 30 min., Hands off: 1 hr.
$^1/_2$ cup olive oil
$^1/_4$ cup dry white wine
2 tablespoons soy sauce
4 (4-ounce) tuna steaks
1 small onion, chopped
1 green bell pepper, chopped
1 medium tomato, chopped
1 garlic clove, minced
$^1/_4$ teaspoon dried crushed red pepper
1 tablespoon olive oil

COMBINE first 3 ingredients in a shallow dish or large zip-top plastic bag; add tuna. Cover or seal, and chill 1 hour, turning occasionally. Remove tuna from marinade, discarding marinade.
GRILL, without grill lid, over medium-high heat (350° to 400°) 3 to 4 minutes on each side or until fish flakes with a fork.
SAUTÉ onion and next 4 ingredients in 1 tablespoon hot oil in a large skillet over medium-high heat until tender. Serve with tuna.

GRILLED SWORDFISH WITH AVOCADO-LIME SAUCE

Makes 4 servings
Hands on: 30 min.
IF YOU CAN'T FIND SWORDFISH, SUBSTITUTE SNAPPER, GROUPER, OR FLOUNDER.

1 lime
1 large avocado
$^3/_4$ cup water
$^1/_2$ teaspoon sea salt, divided
$^1/_2$ teaspoon freshly ground pepper, divided
$^1/_2$ teaspoon ground cumin
$^1/_3$ cup loosely packed fresh cilantro
$^1/_2$ jalapeño pepper
4 garlic cloves
4 (1-inch-thick) swordfish steaks (about $1^1/_2$ pounds)
2 teaspoons olive oil

PEEL lime with a vegetable peeler, reserving green rind only; remove and discard pith. Cut lime into fourths, and place in a blender; add rind.
CUT avocado in half, and scoop pulp into blender; add $^3/_4$ cup water, $^1/_4$ teaspoon salt, $^1/_4$ teaspoon ground pepper, cumin, and next 3 ingredients. Process until sauce is smooth, stopping to scrape down sides. Set sauce aside.
BRUSH fish with oil, and sprinkle with remaining $^1/_4$ teaspoon salt and remaining $^1/_4$ teaspoon ground pepper.
GRILL, covered with grill lid, over high heat (400° to 500°) 5 minutes on each side or until fish flakes with a fork. Serve immediately with sauce. ▶

- Fish should have a fresh smell, not a "fishy" one.
- Choose fillets that appear translucent.
- Avoid fish with bruises and separations in the flesh.
- When in doubt, ask the person at the counter to select the freshest for you.

Sweet-and-spicy Nectarine-Onion Relish tops lightly seasoned Grilled Salmon.

GRILLED SALMON WITH NECTARINE-ONION RELISH

Makes 4 servings
Hands on: 15 min.

4 (6-ounce) salmon fillets
½ teaspoon freshly ground pepper
⅛ teaspoon salt
Nectarine-Onion Relish
Garnish: halved jalapeño pepper

SPRINKLE salmon fillets evenly with pepper and salt.

GRILL fillets, covered with grill lid, over medium-high heat (350° to 400°) 5 minutes on each side or until fish flakes easily with a fork. Serve immediately with relish. Garnish, if desired.

Nectarine-Onion Relish:

Makes 8 cups
Hands on: 20 min., Hands off: 2 hrs.
SAVE THE LEFTOVERS TO TOP GRILLED CHICKEN AND OTHER MEATS.

3 medium nectarines, coarsely chopped
1 red bell pepper, coarsely chopped
1 red onion, coarsely chopped
¼ cup thinly sliced fresh basil
¼ cup white wine vinegar

½ teaspoon grated orange rind
¼ cup fresh orange juice
2 tablespoons seeded and minced jalapeño pepper
2 tablespoons fresh lime juice
2 teaspoons sugar
2 garlic cloves, minced
⅛ teaspoon salt

STIR together chopped nectarines and remaining ingredients in a medium bowl; chill 2 hours.

FISH SKEWERS

Makes 2 to 3 servings
Hands on: 30 min., Hands off: 30 min.

USE ANY COMBINATION OF THESE FISH FILLETS FOR TASTY KABOBS. DOUBLE THE RECIPE FOR A LARGER CROWD.

1 (8-ounce) tuna fillet
1 (8-ounce) grouper fillet
1 (8-ounce) salmon fillet, skinned
4 metal or wooden skewers
1 (8-ounce) bottle olive oil-and-
    vinegar dressing
¼ cup chopped fresh flat-leaf parsley
1 tablespoon fresh rosemary, chopped
1 tablespoon pink peppercorns
2 tablespoons lemon juice

CUT each fish fillet into 1½-inch-thick pieces.

THREAD fish pieces 2 inches apart evenly onto skewers. Place kabobs in a shallow dish.

STIR together olive oil-and-vinegar dressing and next 4 ingredients; pour over fish. Chill 30 minutes.

REMOVE fish from marinade, discarding marinade.

GRILL, covered with grill lid, over high heat (400° to 500°) 4 minutes on each side or until fish reaches desired degree of doneness.

NOTE: If using wooden skewers, soak in water 30 minutes beforehand to prevent burning.

PASTA WITH WHITE CLAM SAUCE

Makes 6 servings
Hands on: 30 min.

2 (10-ounce) cans baby clams,
    undrained
6 garlic cloves, sliced
2 tablespoons olive oil
1 (8-ounce) bottle clam juice
1 teaspoon dried basil
½ to ¾ teaspoon dried crushed red
    pepper
¼ cup lemon juice
6 cups hot cooked linguine (12 ounces
    uncooked)
½ cup chopped fresh parsley
1 teaspoon grated lemon rind
½ teaspoon salt
¼ teaspoon black pepper
½ cup shredded Parmesan cheese

DRAIN clams, reserving juice.

SAUTÉ garlic in hot oil over medium heat in a small saucepan 2 minutes. Stir in re-

Shrimp With Cilantro and Lime is tossed with a mildly spiced citrus mixture and served over hot angel hair pasta.

SHRIMP WITH CILANTRO AND LIME

Makes 4 servings
Hands on: 30 min.

2 pounds unpeeled, large fresh
    shrimp
¼ cup fresh lime juice
½ teaspoon ground cumin
¼ teaspoon ground ginger
4 garlic cloves, minced
2 tablespoons olive oil
¼ cup chopped fresh cilantro
2 teaspoons grated lime rind
½ teaspoon salt
½ teaspoon pepper
Hot cooked angel hair pasta
Garnishes: chopped fresh cilantro,
    lime wedges

PEEL shrimp, and devein, if desired. Toss together shrimp, lime juice, and next 3 ingredients.

SAUTÉ shrimp mixture in hot oil in a large nonstick skillet over medium-high heat, 4 minutes or just until shrimp turn pink. Remove from heat; stir in cilantro and next 3 ingredients. Serve immediately over pasta. Garnish, if desired

served clam juice, bottled clam juice, basil, and red pepper; bring to a boil. Reduce heat, and simmer 3 minutes; add clams and lemon juice, and cook 3 minutes or until thoroughly heated.

TOSS together pasta, clam sauce, parsley, and next 3 ingredients. Sprinkle with Parmesan cheese.

SHRIMP-TOMATO PASTA

Makes 4 servings
Hands on: 30 min.

TO SAVE TIME, USE PREPACKAGED, UNCOOKED, FROZEN, PEELED SHRIMP FOUND IN THE FREEZER SECTION. THAW ACCORDING TO PACKAGE DIRECTIONS, AND PROCEED AS DIRECTED.

10 ounces uncooked fettuccine
1 pound unpeeled, medium-size fresh
    shrimp
3 tomatoes, peeled and chopped
6 to 8 fresh mushrooms, sliced
2 green onions, sliced
¼ cup sliced ripe olives
¼ cup dry white wine
1 tablespoon dried Italian seasoning
1 tablespoon olive oil
¼ teaspoon salt
¼ teaspoon lemon pepper seasoning
¼ teaspoon ground black pepper
⅛ teaspoon ground red pepper
¼ teaspoon capers
2 tablespoons grated Parmesan
    cheese

COOK pasta according to package directions; drain and keep warm.

PEEL shrimp; devein, if desired.

BRING shrimp, tomatoes, and next 11 ingredients to a boil in a skillet. Reduce heat; simmer, stirring occasionally, 5 minutes or just until shrimp turn pink and sauce is slightly thickened. Serve over fettuccine, and sprinkle with grated Parmesan cheese.   ◆

Breakfast always makes a scrumptious plate, whether it's morning, noon, or night. For something out of the ordinary, make one of these fabulous dishes. Serve with hash browns or a side of fresh fruit.

Breakfast Anytime

TRADITIONAL EGGS BENEDICT

Makes 2 servings
Hands on: 20 min.

8 (¹/₂-ounce) Canadian bacon slices
Vegetable cooking spray
2 English muffins, split and toasted
4 large eggs, poached
Hollandaise Sauce
Garnishes: paprika and coarsely ground pepper
Fresh fruit, fresh mint sprig (optional)

COOK bacon in a skillet coated with cooking spray over medium heat until thoroughly heated, turning once. Drain on paper towels.
PLACE 2 bacon slices on each muffin half. Top each with a poached egg, and drizzle evenly with Hollandaise Sauce; garnish, if desired. Serve immediately with fresh fruit and mint sprig, if desired.

Hollandaise Sauce:

Makes 1¹/₂ cups
Hands on: 20 min.

4 egg yolks
2 tablespoons fresh lemon juice
1 cup butter, melted
¹/₄ teaspoon salt

WHISK yolks in top of a double boiler; gradually whisk in lemon juice. Place over hot water. (Do not boil.) Add butter, ¹/₃ cup at a time, whisking until smooth; whisk in salt. Cook, whisking constantly, 10 minutes or until thickened and a thermometer registers 160°. Use immediately.

Homemade Hollandaise Sauce is drizzled over Traditional Eggs Benedict.

Banana Pancakes

Makes 9 pancakes
Hands on: 30 min.

1 cup all-purpose flour
1 tablespoon sugar
1 teaspoon baking powder
½ teaspoon baking soda
¼ teaspoon salt
1¼ cups buttermilk
1 large egg
1 tablespoon vegetable oil
½ teaspoon vanilla extract
1½ cups chopped ripe banana
Cinnamon-Vanilla Syrup
3 tablespoons chopped pecans,
   toasted

STIR together first 5 ingredients; make a well in center of mixture.
WHISK together buttermilk and next 3 ingredients; add to dry ingredients, stirring just until moistened. Fold in banana.
POUR about ⅓ cup batter for each pancake onto a hot, lightly greased griddle. Cook pancakes until tops are covered with bubbles and edges look cooked; turn and cook other side. Serve pancakes with Cinnamon-Vanilla Syrup, and sprinkle with pecans.

Cinnamon-Vanilla Syrup:

Makes ¾ cup
Hands on: 5 min.

¾ cup light corn syrup
½ teaspoon ground cinnamon
1 teaspoon vanilla extract
½ teaspoon lemon juice

WHISK together ¾ cup corn syrup and remaining ingredients.

Ham-and-Cheese Omelet

Makes 2 omelets
Hands on: 30 min.

HAVARTI, A CREAMY, BUTTERY-FLAVORED CHEESE, IS A NICE UPDATE TO THE TRADITIONAL OMELET. IF YOU CAN'T FIND HAVARTI, USE GOUDA OR SWISS CHEESE INSTEAD.

6 large eggs
2 tablespoons chopped fresh chives
¼ teaspoon salt
¼ teaspoon pepper
Vegetable cooking spray
2 teaspoons butter or margarine,
   divided
1 cup chopped smoked ham
½ cup shredded Havarti cheese
4 (1-ounce) Swiss cheese slices

WHISK together first 4 ingredients.
MELT 1 teaspoon butter in a small non-stick skillet coated with cooking spray over medium-high heat, rotating pan to coat bottom evenly.
ADD half of egg mixture to skillet. As egg mixture starts to cook, gently lift edges of omelet with a spatula, and tilt pan so uncooked portion flows underneath. Cook 3 minutes or until almost set. Flip omelet over.
TOP 1 side of omelet with half each of ham and cheeses. Fold in half. Cook 1 to 2 minutes or until cheese melts. Remove from pan, and keep warm. Repeat procedure with remaining 1 teaspoon butter, egg mixture, ham, and cheeses to make next omelet. Serve immediately.

Maple-Pecan Sauce

Makes 1¼ cups
Hands on: 15 min.

SERVE THIS SWEET SAUCE OVER WAFFLES, FRENCH TOAST, OR PANCAKES.

1 cup maple syrup
¼ cup honey
½ cup chopped pecans, toasted
¼ teaspoon ground cinnamon

COOK syrup and honey in a small saucepan over medium heat, stirring often, 10 minutes or until slightly thickened. Remove from heat; stir in pecans and cinnamon. (Mixture will thicken as it cools.)

Open-Faced Bacon-and-Potato Omelet

Makes 2 servings
Hands on: 45 min.

4 bacon slices, chopped
2 cups frozen Southern-style cubed
   hash browns, thawed
4 green onions, thinly sliced
2 teaspoons butter or margarine
1 large tomato, seeded and chopped
2 tablespoons chopped fresh Italian
   parsley
6 large eggs
½ teaspoon salt
¼ teaspoon pepper
4 drops hot sauce (optional)
1 cup shredded sharp Cheddar cheese

COOK bacon in a large ovenproof non-stick skillet over medium heat until crisp; remove bacon, and drain on paper towels, reserving 1 tablespoon drippings in skillet. Set bacon aside.
COOK hash browns in hot drippings over medium heat 10 minutes or until hash browns are tender, stirring occasionally. Stir in green onions; cook 5 minutes or until tender.
ADD butter to skillet, stirring until melted. Add tomato, and cook over medium-high heat 3 to 4 minutes.
SPRINKLE with bacon and parsley.
WHISK together eggs, salt, pepper, and, if desired, hot sauce. Pour over hash

(recipe continues on page 69)

poaching eggs

Add water to a depth of 3 inches to a large saucepan. Bring to a boil; reduce heat, and maintain at a light simmer. Add ½ teaspoon vinegar. Break eggs and slip into water, one at a time, as close as possible to surface of water. Simmer 3 to 5 minutes or to desired degree of doneness. Remove eggs with a slotted spoon. Trim edges, if desired.

Creamy Shrimp Sauce smothers fresh asparagus over grits cakes in Shrimp-and-Grits Eggs Benedict.

SHRIMP-AND-GRITS EGGS BENEDICT

Makes 8 servings
Hands on: 30 min.; Hands off: 8 hrs., 8 min.

THIS RECIPE MAY SEEM LIKE IT HAS A LOT OF STEPS, BUT THE FLAVOR IS WELL WORTH IT. THE GRITS ARE MADE THE DAY BEFORE.

5 cups water
1/2 teaspoon salt
1 cup uncooked quick-cooking grits
1/2 teaspoon pepper
3/4 cup freshly grated Parmesan cheese
1 pound fresh asparagus
1/3 cup all-purpose flour
1 tablespoon butter or margarine
1 tablespoon vegetable oil
8 large eggs, poached
Creamy Shrimp Sauce
Garnish: freshly grated Parmesan cheese

BRING 5 cups water and salt to a boil in a medium saucepan; gradually stir in grits. Cook over medium heat 8 minutes or until thickened.
WHISK in pepper and cheese; spoon into a lightly greased 11- x 7-inch baking dish. Cover and chill 8 hours.

SNAP off tough ends of asparagus; use a vegetable peeler to remove scales, if desired. Combine asparagus and water to cover in a saucepan. Bring to a boil, and cook 5 minutes or until crisp-tender. Drain and plunge asparagus into ice water to stop the cooking process; set aside.
CUT grits into 8 squares. Lightly dredge in flour.
MELT butter with oil in a large nonstick skillet over medium-low heat. Cook grits squares, in batches, 3 to 4 minutes on each side or until golden.
TOP each square with asparagus, a poached egg, and Creamy Shrimp Sauce; garnish, if desired. Serve immediately.

Creamy Shrimp Sauce:
Makes 2 1/4 cups
Hands on: 25 min., Hands off: 30 min.

1 pound unpeeled, medium-size fresh shrimp
2 1/2 tablespoons butter, divided
1 small shallot, sliced
1 (14-ounce) can chicken broth
1 1/2 tablespoons all-purpose flour
1 cup whipping cream
2 tablespoons sherry

PEEL shrimp, reserving shells; devein, if desired.
MELT 1 tablespoon butter in a 3 1/2-quart saucepan over medium heat. Add shrimp, and cook 5 minutes or just until shrimp turn pink. Chop shrimp, and set aside.
ADD shrimp shells, shallot, and chicken broth to saucepan; bring to a boil. Remove from heat, cover, and let stand 30 minutes. Pour broth mixture through a wire-mesh strainer into a bowl, discarding shells and shallot.
MELT remaining 1 1/2 tablespoons butter in saucepan over medium heat. Whisk in flour. Cook, whisking constantly, 1 minute. Gradually whisk in chicken broth mixture. Bring to a boil; boil 1 minute or until slightly thickened. Add whipping cream; reduce heat to low. Add chopped shrimp and sherry, and stir until thoroughly heated.

(continued from page 67)
brown mixture. Gently lift edges of omelet, and tilt pan so uncooked portion flows underneath. Cook over medium heat until omelet begins to set. Sprinkle with cheese.

BROIL 5½ inches from heat 5 minutes or until top is set and cheese melts. Slide out of skillet onto platter. Cut into wedges, and serve immediately.

BLUEBERRY PANCAKES

Makes 8 to 10 pancakes
Hands on: 30 min.
1½ cups all-purpose flour
¼ cup sugar
1 teaspoon baking powder
⅛ teaspoon salt
¾ cup milk
1 large egg
1 tablespoon vegetable oil
½ cup fresh or frozen blueberries
Maple syrup

STIR together first 4 ingredients; make a well in center of mixture.

STIR together milk, egg, and oil; add to dry ingredients, stirring just until moistened. Fold in blueberries.

POUR about ¼ cup batter for each pancake onto a hot, lightly greased griddle. Cook pancakes until tops are covered with bubbles and edges look cooked; turn and cook other side. Serve with maple syrup.

SMOTHERED HASH BROWNS

Makes 8 servings
Hands on: 30 min.
PRESSING DOWN FIRMLY ON HASH BROWNS WITH A SPATULA WILL HELP KEEP THEM FROM FALLING APART. ADD YOUR FAVORITE TOPPINGS, SUCH AS CHOPPED TOMATOES, DICED ONIONS, AND EVEN CHILI.

1 medium onion, diced
3 tablespoons vegetable oil, divided
1 (16-ounce) package frozen shredded hash browns, thawed
1 teaspoon salt
½ teaspoon pepper
8 American cheese slices

SAUTÉ onion in 1 tablespoon hot vegetable oil over medium heat 8 minutes or until tender.

STIR together onion, hash browns, salt, and pepper in a large bowl.

HEAT 1 tablespoon oil in a large nonstick skillet over medium-high heat. Drop hash brown mixture into skillet to form 3½-inch rounds. Cook, in batches, 5 minutes on each side or until lightly browned, adding remaining oil as necessary. Press down with a spatula to flatten; top each round with a cheese slice. Cook 5 minutes.

SPANISH OMELET WITH FRESH AVOCADO SALSA

Makes 2 omelets
Hands on: 30 min.
1 cup chopped chorizo sausage (about 4 ounces)*
1 small sweet onion, chopped
½ small green bell pepper, chopped
1 garlic clove, minced
6 large eggs
¼ teaspoon salt
¼ teaspoon pepper
Vegetable cooking spray
2 teaspoons butter, divided
1 (3-ounce) package goat cheese, crumbled
Fresh Avocado Salsa
Toppings: sour cream, freshly ground pepper

COOK first 4 ingredients in a small nonstick skillet over medium-high heat 10 minutes or until vegetables are tender. Remove sausage mixture from skillet, and set aside. Wipe skillet clean.

WHISK together eggs, salt, and pepper.

MELT 1 teaspoon butter in skillet coated with cooking spray over medium-high heat, rotating skillet to coat bottom evenly. Add half of egg mixture. As egg mixture starts to cook, gently lift edges of omelet with a spatula, and tilt pan so uncooked portion flows underneath. Flip omelet over.

SPRINKLE 1 side of omelet with half each of chorizo mixture and goat cheese. Fold over omelet; remove from pan, and keep warm. Repeat procedure with remaining 1 teaspoon butter, egg mixture, chorizo mixture, and cheese. Serve immediately with Fresh Avocado Salsa and desired toppings.

*Spicy smoked sausage may be substituted for chorizo.

Fresh Avocado Salsa:
Makes about 2 cups
Hands on: 15 min.
4 plum tomatoes, chopped
1 small sweet onion, chopped
1 small jalapeño pepper, seeded and minced
¼ cup chopped fresh cilantro
2 tablespoons fresh lime juice
½ teaspoon salt
1 small avocado, chopped

TOSS together first 6 ingredients. Cover and chill until ready to serve. Toss in avocado just before serving.

NOTE: For best results, serve salsa within 4 hours.

CREAMY VEGGIE OMELET

Makes 2 omelets
Hands on: 30 min.
6 large eggs
¼ teaspoon salt
¼ teaspoon pepper
4 teaspoons butter or margarine, divided
Vegetable cooking spray
½ small red bell pepper, chopped
½ small green bell pepper, chopped
1 cup sliced fresh mushrooms
1 cup chopped fresh broccoli
¼ teaspoon salt
¼ teaspoon pepper
3 tablespoons soft chive-and-onion cream cheese
3 tablespoons crumbled feta cheese*

WHISK together eggs, ¼ teaspoon salt, and ¼ teaspoon pepper; set aside.

MELT 2 teaspoons butter in a small, heavy nonstick skillet coated with cooking spray over medium-high heat, rotating pan to coat bottom evenly. Add red bell pepper and next 5 ingredients. Cook, stirring often, 10 minutes or until peppers are tender. Remove mixture from skillet; set aside.

WIPE skillet clean, and coat with cooking spray.

RETURN to heat. Melt 1 teaspoon butter in skillet over medium-high heat; add half of egg mixture. As egg mixture starts to cook, gently lift edges of omelet with a spatula, and tilt pan so uncooked portion flows underneath. Flip omelet over.

SPRINKLE 1 side of omelet with half of vegetable mixture. Dollop with half of cream cheese, and sprinkle with half of feta cheese; fold omelet in half. Cook 2 minutes or until cheese melts. Remove from pan, and keep warm. Repeat with remaining 1 teaspoon butter, egg mixture, vegetable mixture, and cheeses. Serve immediately.

*¼ cup shredded Swiss cheese may be substituted. ◆

Fresh Salads for Supper

Shrimp-and-Asparagus Salad With Spicy Ranch Dressing is perfect for a springtime gathering.

If a heavy entrée is not what you fancy, try any one of these main-dish salads. Enjoy the flavors of seasoned grilled meats, zesty dressings, and toppings galore, and round out the meal with Blue Cheese Bread or Parmesan Toasts. When shopping, remember that the greener the lettuce, the better for you it is. Use fresh spinach and other dark salad greens for an even more nutritious meal.

BACON, MOZZARELLA, AND TOMATO SALAD

Makes 4 to 6 servings
Hands on: 30 min.

1 (16-ounce) bottle balsamic vinaigrette
1/3 cup lime juice
8 ounces mozzarella cheese, cut into 1/4-inch-thick slices
1 (16-ounce) unsliced French or Italian bread loaf
1 large head Bibb lettuce
6 plum tomatoes, cut into 1/4-inch-thick slices
12 thick bacon slices, cut into thirds and cooked

STIR together vinaigrette and lime juice. Place cheese slices in a 13- x 9-inch dish. Drizzle with 1 cup vinaigrette mixture. Let stand 20 minutes.
SLICE off top one-fourth of bread loaf.

Scoop out bread, leaving a 1-inch-thick shell. (Reserve top and center for another use, if desired.) Place shell on a baking sheet, and brush inside with 1/2 cup vinaigrette mixture.
BAKE at 400° for 12 to 15 minutes or until golden; cool. Line bread shell with lettuce. Fill with tomatoes and cheese; top with bacon. Serve with remaining vinaigrette mixture.

ITALIAN BREAD SALAD

Makes 4 servings
Hands on: 30 min., Hands off: 15 min.
FOR MORE FLAVOR, SUBSTITUTE 1 CUP THINLY SLICED SALAMI STRIPS FOR 2 CUPS HAM.

4 cups cubed French bread
6 tablespoons olive oil
3 tablespoons red wine vinegar

2 garlic cloves, minced
1 teaspoon dried oregano
1 teaspoon salt
3/4 teaspoon freshly ground black pepper
1/8 to 1/4 teaspoon dried crushed red pepper
1 large head romaine lettuce, chopped
4 to 5 large plum tomatoes, chopped
2 cups chopped smoked ham
1 (8-ounce) package fresh mozzarella cheese, cubed
3 green onions, chopped

PLACE bread cubes on a baking sheet.
BAKE at 325° for 15 minutes or until toasted. Set bread cubes aside.
WHISK together olive oil and next 6 ingredients.
RESERVE 1 cup toasted bread cubes. Scatter remaining cubes on a large serving platter. Top with lettuce and next 3 ingredients. Drizzle with dressing 15 minutes before serving, and toss. Sprinkle with reserved bread cubes and chopped green onions.

BLUE CHEESE BREAD

Makes 8 servings
Hands on: 10 min., Hands off: 7 min.
THE STRONG FLAVOR AND AROMA OF THIS TOASTED BREAD IS A NICE COMPLEMENT TO MANY OF THE SALADS FOUND HERE.

1 (12-ounce) crusty French bread loaf
1/2 cup butter, softened
1 (4-ounce) package crumbled blue cheese

CUT French bread loaf into 3/4-inch-thick slices, cutting to, but not through, opposite side.
STIR together 1/2 cup butter and crumbled blue cheese; spread evenly on both sides of each bread slice. Wrap bread loaf in aluminum foil, and place on a baking sheet.
BAKE at 375° for 7 minutes or until bread is toasted.

SHRIMP-AND-ASPARAGUS SALAD WITH SPICY RANCH DRESSING

Makes 8 servings
Hands on: 45 min.

2 pounds unpeeled large fresh shrimp
12 cups water
2 pounds fresh asparagus
8 cups gourmet salad greens
3 large yellow tomatoes, sliced
1 pint cherry tomatoes
1 small red onion, diced
1 small red bell pepper, diced
1 (4-ounce) package feta cheese with garlic and herbs, crumbled
Spicy Ranch Dressing

PEEL shrimp, and devein, if desired. Bring 12 cups water to a boil; add shrimp, and cook 3 to 5 minutes or just until shrimp turn pink. Drain and rinse with cold water; chill.
SNAP off and discard tough ends of asparagus, and remove scales with a vegetable peeler, if desired. Cook in boiling water to cover 1 minute or until crisp-tender; drain. Plunge into ice water to

stop the cooking process; drain.
PLACE salad greens on a large platter. Arrange asparagus, shrimp, and tomatoes over greens. Sprinkle with onion, bell pepper, and cheese. Serve with Spicy Ranch Dressing.

Spicy Ranch Dressing:
Makes 3 cups
Hands on: 10 min., Hands off: 30 min.

2 cups mayonnaise
1/2 cup buttermilk
1 (0.4-ounce) envelope buttermilk Ranch dressing mix
4 green onions, sliced
1/4 cup fresh chopped basil
1/4 cup fresh lemon juice
1/2 teaspoon ground red pepper

WHISK together 2 cups mayonnaise and remaining ingredients. Chill 30 minutes.

SPICY CHICKEN SALAD

Makes 4 servings
Hands on: 35 min.

3 cups chopped tomato
¾ cup diced yellow bell pepper
¼ cup diced red onion
1 tablespoon sugar
3 tablespoons cider vinegar
½ teaspoon salt
¼ teaspoon pepper
5 tablespoons olive oil, divided
¼ cup lemon juice
¼ cup Dijon mustard
1 tablespoon honey
4 skinned and boned chicken breasts
3 tablespoons Spicy Seasoning
1 pound sugar snap peas, trimmed
8 cups torn romaine lettuce

TOSS together first 7 ingredients in a bowl; cover tomato mixture, and chill.
WHISK together 3 tablespoons oil, lemon juice, mustard, and honey in a large bowl; cover mustard mixture, and chill.
RUB chicken with Spicy Seasoning.
COOK chicken in remaining 2 tablespoons oil in a large heavy skillet over medium-high heat 7 minutes on each side or until done. Remove from skillet, and cool. Cut chicken into thin strips, and set aside.
ARRANGE sugar snap peas in a steamer basket over boiling water; cover and steam 2 minutes or until crisp-tender. Plunge into ice water to stop the cooking process, and drain.
TOSS peas and lettuce with mustard mixture. Top each serving evenly with tomato mixture and chicken strips.

Spicy Seasoning:

Makes about ½ cup
Hands on: 5 min.

USE THIS FLAVORFUL RUB TO SEASON FISH, POULTRY, MEATS, AND ASSORTED VEGETABLES.

2½ tablespoons paprika
2 tablespoons garlic powder
1 tablespoon salt
1 tablespoon onion powder
1 tablespoon dried thyme
1 tablespoon ground red pepper
1 tablespoon ground black pepper

STIR together all ingredients. Store in an airtight container.

CHUTNEY CURRIED TURKEY SALAD

Makes 5 cups
Hands on: 15 min.

½ cup sour cream
½ cup mayonnaise
¼ cup mango chutney
1 tablespoon grated orange rind
2 tablespoons fresh orange juice
1 teaspoon salt
1 to 2 teaspoons curry powder
½ teaspoon pepper
4 cups cubed cooked turkey
½ small red onion, thinly sliced
3 green onions, chopped
1 (8-ounce) can sliced water
 chestnuts, rinsed and drained
½ cup slivered almonds, toasted
Spinach leaves

STIR together first 8 ingredients in a large bowl. Add turkey and next 4 ingredients; toss well. Cover and chill 3 hours, if desired. Serve on spinach-lined plates.

COUSCOUS-PORK SALAD

Makes 6 servings
Hands on: 30 min.; Hands off: 2 hrs., 25 min.

2 cups water
1 cup uncooked couscous
⅓ cup olive oil
⅓ cup lemon juice
½ teaspoon salt
¼ teaspoon ground cumin
¼ teaspoon curry powder
¼ teaspoon coarsely ground pepper
2 cups shredded cooked pork or
 chicken
1 cup seeded, coarsely chopped
 cucumber
½ cup shredded carrot
½ cup thinly sliced radishes
⅓ cup sliced green onions
¼ cup chopped fresh parsley

BRING 2 cups water to a boil in a medium saucepan. Stir in couscous. Cover, and remove from heat. Let stand 5 minutes or until liquid is absorbed. Fluff couscous with a fork; let cool 20 minutes.
WHISK together olive oil and next 5 ingredients in a large bowl; add couscous, pork, and remaining ingredients to olive oil mixture, tossing gently. Chill at least 2 hours.

TUNA-AND-WHITE BEAN SALAD

Makes 3 to 4 servings
Hands on: 20 min., Hands off: 2 hrs.

1 small sweet onion, diced
½ cup olive oil
¼ cup red wine vinegar
¼ cup chopped fresh parsley
2 tablespoons chopped fresh or
 2 teaspoons dried basil
2 teaspoons sugar
1 teaspoon garlic salt
¾ teaspoon pepper
3 tablespoons lemon juice
2 (15½-ounce) cans white beans,
 rinsed and drained
1 (12-ounce) can solid white tuna in
 spring water, drained and broken
 into chunks
Lettuce leaves
Tomato wedges (optional)

WHISK together first 9 ingredients in a medium bowl; add beans and tuna, tossing gently. Cover and chill at least 2 hours. Serve on lettuce-lined plates; top with tomato wedges, if desired. ▶

STEAK SALAD NIÇOISE

Makes 4 servings
Hands on: 30 min.; Hands off: 1 hr., 5 min.

1 (16-ounce) bottle vinaigrette
2 tablespoons Dijon mustard
2 teaspoons anchovy paste
 (optional)
1½ pounds flank steak
4 medium-size new potatoes, cut
 into ¼-inch-thick slices
¼ pound small green beans,
 trimmed
4 plum tomatoes, each cut into 4
 wedges
16 kalamata or ripe black olives
2 hard-cooked eggs, quartered
 (optional)
6 cups gourmet salad greens

WHISK together vinaigrette, mustard, and, if desired, anchovy paste.
POUR ½ cup vinaigrette mixture into a shallow dish or zip-top plastic freezer bag; add flank steak. Cover or seal, and chill 1 hour, turning occasionally. Reserve remaining vinaigrette mixture.
COOK potatoes in boiling water to cover in a large saucepan 10 minutes; add green beans, and cook 5 minutes or until beans are crisp-tender. Drain and rinse with cold water to stop the cooking process.
REMOVE flank steak from marinade; discard marinade.
GRILL steak, covered with grill lid, over medium-high heat (350° to 400°) 5 minutes on each side or to desired degree of doneness. Remove from grill, and let stand 5 minutes. Cut steak diagonally across the grain into ¼-inch-thick slices.
ARRANGE steak, green beans, potatoes, tomatoes, olives, and, if desired, eggs on salad greens. Serve with reserved vinaigrette mixture.

speedy salads

Use these time-saving tips to get supper on the table fast.
■ Grill or bake extra chicken breasts, and freeze for later use.
■ Chop and freeze baked ham to have on hand for salads and casseroles.
■ Chop raw vegetables for salads, and store them separately in zip-top plastic bags. Chill up to 2 days.
■ Prepare dressings up to 2 days in advance. Just whisk before serving.

CHEF'S SALAD

Makes 6 servings
Hands on: 20 min.

8 cups mixed salad greens
2 cups mixed chopped fresh vegetables
1 small red onion, sliced
3 cups chopped cooked chicken
1 large avocado, peeled and sliced
6 bacon slices, cooked and crumbled
3 cups croutons
1 (16-ounce) bottle Ranch dressing

TOSS first 3 ingredients. Top with chicken and avocado slices, and sprinkle with bacon and croutons. Serve with Ranch dressing.

NOTE: For mixed chopped fresh vegetables, we used yellow squash, cucumber, broccoli, red bell pepper, and carrots. You can use any of your favorites.

Greek Chicken Salad

Makes 4 to 6 servings
Hands on: 15 min.

3 cups shredded romaine lettuce
2 cups chopped cooked chicken
1 cup canned garbanzo beans, drained
2 tomatoes, cut into wedges
¾ cup kalamata olives, pitted
Lemon-Herb Dressing
1 (4-ounce) package crumbled feta cheese
Toasted pita bread triangles

COMBINE first 5 ingredients in a large salad bowl. Toss with Lemon-Herb Dressing; top with feta cheese. Serve with toasted pita bread triangles.

Lemon-Herb Dressing:

Makes ¾ cup
Hands on: 10 min., Hands off: 1 hr.
TRY THIS TANGY DRESSING ON ANY TOSSED SALAD.

3 tablespoons lemon juice
½ cup olive oil
1 tablespoon chopped fresh mint
1 tablespoon chopped fresh oregano
1 tablespoon chopped fresh parsley
½ teaspoon salt
½ teaspoon pepper

WHISK together all ingredients until well blended; chill at least 1 hour.

Roast Beef-Blue Cheese Salad

Makes 4 servings
Hands on: 10 min.

8 ounces thinly sliced roast beef
1 pint cherry tomatoes
1 (8.5-ounce) package mixed salad greens
¼ cup (1 ounce) crumbled blue cheese or feta cheese
¼ cup olive oil vinaigrette
Parmesan Toasts

ARRANGE roast beef slices into 2 stacks; roll up stacks. Cut into 1-inch slices. Arrange beef and tomatoes over salad greens. Sprinkle with blue cheese, and drizzle with olive oil vinaigrette. Serve with Parmesan Toasts.

Parmesan Toasts:

Makes 4 servings
Hands on: 10 min.

4 Italian bread slices
1 tablespoon butter or margarine, melted
¼ cup freshly grated Parmesan cheese
¼ teaspoon freshly ground pepper

BRUSH each bread slice evenly with butter. Sprinkle evenly with cheese and pepper. Place on a baking sheet.
BROIL 3½ inches from heat 3 minutes or until lightly browned.

Grilled Chicken With Lemon-Yogurt Coleslaw

Makes 4 servings
Hands on: 20 min., Hands off: 16 min.

4 skinned and boned chicken breasts
½ teaspoon garlic salt
1 teaspoon lemon pepper seasoning
½ cup plain yogurt
1 tablespoon sugar
2 tablespoons lemon juice
½ cup crumbled feta cheese
2 tablespoons minced fresh chives
1 (10-ounce) package finely shredded cabbage

SPRINKLE chicken with garlic salt and lemon pepper.
GRILL chicken breasts, covered with grill lid, over medium-high heat (350° to 400°) 7 to 8 minutes on each side or until done. Cool slightly, and cut into thin strips.
WHISK together yogurt and next 4 ingredients, and toss with cabbage. Serve chicken strips over coleslaw. ◆

Fruity Chicken Salad

Makes 6 to 8 servings
Hands on: 20 min.

IT'S BEST TO CHILL DRESSING FOR AT LEAST AN HOUR TO LET FLAVORS FULLY BLEND.

¾ cup sugar
⅓ cup red wine vinegar
1 teaspoon salt
1 teaspoon dry mustard
1 teaspoon grated onion
1 cup vegetable oil
1 tablespoon poppy seeds (optional)
3 cups chopped cooked chicken
6 cups torn fresh spinach
1 quart strawberries, sliced
3 kiwifruit, peeled and sliced
1 cup sliced almonds, toasted

PROCESS first 5 ingredients in blender until smooth, stopping to scrape down sides.
TURN blender on high; add oil in a slow, steady stream. Pour mixture into a serving bowl, and stir in poppy seeds, if desired. Toss together chicken and dressing; chill until ready to serve.
PLACE spinach on individual serving plates; top with fruit, chicken mixture, and almonds.

Better on a Bun

Cubes of Monterey Jack cheese are sealed between two seasoned beef patties for a melted surprise in Stuffed Southwestern Burgers.

Nothing beats a burger—especially one with the works. Sample some new twists on this old standby with seasoned meats, cheesy fillings, and flavorful spreads. See our helpful suggestions for the ultimate burger menu.

MOZZARELLA-BASIL BURGERS

Makes 8 servings
Hands on: 25 min.

1/2 cup mayonnaise
1 garlic clove, pressed
2 pounds lean ground beef
1/2 cup Italian-seasoned
    breadcrumbs
2 large eggs, lightly beaten
3 tablespoons ketchup
1 (6-ounce) package mozzarella
    cheese slices
8 hamburger buns, split
24 large fresh basil leaves
Toppings: tomato slices, red onion
    slices

STIR together 1/2 cup mayonnaise and garlic; set aside.
COMBINE ground beef and next 3 ingredients. Shape into 8 patties.
GRILL patties, covered with grill lid, over medium-high heat (350° to 400°) 5 minutes on each side or until done. Top each patty with a cheese slice.
PLACE buns, cut sides down, on grill rack, and grill until lightly browned. Spread mayonnaise mixture on cut sides

of buns; top each bottom half with 3 basil leaves, beef patty, desired toppings, and top halves of buns.

SALMON BURGERS

Makes 6 servings
Hands on: 30 min.

3 (6-ounce) cans skinless boneless
    pink salmon, undrained
1 (8-ounce) package Italian-seasoned
    breadcrumbs
1 (8-ounce) carton egg substitute
    (1 cup)
1/3 cup lemon juice
1 teaspoon salt
1 teaspoon paprika
2 tablespoons vegetable oil
6 sourdough English muffins, split and
    toasted
Alfalfa sprouts

COMBINE first 6 ingredients; shape into 6 patties. Cook, in batches, in hot oil in a large nonstick skillet over medium heat 5 minutes on each side or until done. Drain on paper towels.
SERVE on toasted English muffins with alfalfa sprouts.

JALAPEÑO CHEESEBURGERS

Makes 6 servings
Hands on: 25 min.

2 pounds ground chuck
1/2 teaspoon salt
1/2 teaspoon pepper
1 (3-ounce) package cream cheese,
    softened
1 tablespoon grated onion
1 to 2 jalapeño peppers, seeded and
    minced
6 sandwich buns
Toppings: lettuce leaves, red onion
    slices, tomato slices

COMBINE first 3 ingredients; shape into 12 thin patties.
STIR together cream cheese, onion, and jalapeño peppers; spoon evenly in center of 6 patties. (Do not spread to edges.) Top with remaining patties, pressing edges to seal.
GRILL patties, covered with grill lid, over medium-high heat (350° to 400°) 5 minutes on each side or until done. Serve on buns with desired toppings.

GRILLED PORTOBELLO BURGERS

Makes 6 servings
Hands on: 20 min., Hands off: 20 min.

6 large portobello mushroom caps
1/2 cup teriyaki sauce
6 (1-ounce) slices mozzarella cheese
1/4 cup mayonnaise
6 sourdough buns, split

COMBINE mushroom caps and teriyaki sauce in a zip-top plastic bag, turning to coat; seal and let stand 20 minutes. Drain mushrooms, discarding marinade.
GRILL mushrooms, covered with grill lid, over medium-high heat (350° to 400°) 2 minutes on each side. Top with cheese, and grill 2 minutes.
SPREAD mayonnaise on cut sides of buns. Grill buns, cut sides down, 1 minute or until toasted. Place mushrooms in buns, and serve immediately.
NOTE: For testing purposes only, we used Kikkoman Teriyaki Sauce. ▶

STUFFED SOUTHWESTERN BURGERS

Makes 6 servings
Hands on: 40 min.

1 avocado
3 plum tomatoes, chopped
1 garlic clove, pressed
2 teaspoons lemon juice
1 1/2 teaspoons salt, divided
1 1/2 teaspoons pepper, divided
2 pounds lean ground beef
1 small onion, finely chopped
2 teaspoons chili powder
1 (8-ounce) block Monterey Jack
    cheese with peppers, cubed
6 large sesame seed buns, toasted
Toppings: leaf lettuce, tomato slices,
    red onion slices

MASH avocado with a fork; stir in

chopped tomatoes, garlic, lemon juice, 1/2 teaspoon salt, and 1/2 teaspoon pepper. Set aside.
COMBINE ground beef, onion, remaining 1 teaspoon salt, remaining 1 teaspoon pepper, and chili powder; shape into 12 thin patties.
TOP 6 patties with cheese cubes; cover with remaining patties, pressing edges to seal.
GRILL patties, covered with grill lid, over medium-high heat (350° to 400°) 5 minutes on each side or until done. Serve in buns with desired toppings and avocado mixture.

Kid-size portions make Mini-Cheeseburgers a lunch favorite.

burger basics

■ Rescue hands from the messy mixing of ground meats by combining patty ingredients in a zip-top plastic freezer bag; squeeze just until combined. Wearing latex gloves while mixing is another way to keep your hands clean.

■ For consistent patty sizes, use a large spoon or ice-cream scoop to measure the meat mixture.

■ Keep the meat from sticking to your fingers by wetting your hands with water while forming the burger patties.

■ Allow patties to be a little loose rather than heavily packed. Compacted meat patties produce a dense, solid burger.

■ For moist and juicy burgers, look for a coarse grind of meat. Avoid finely ground beef.

■ Raw ground beef can be frozen up to 3 months in the freezer or stored up to 2 days in the refrigerator.

■ When grilling, resist the temptation to press the burgers flat. You'll squeeze all the flavorful juices out.

Herbed Onion-Turkey Burgers

Makes 8 servings
Hands on: 25 min.

2 pounds ground turkey
$1/3$ cup mayonnaise
1 (1-ounce) envelope dry onion soup mix
1 tablespoon minced fresh or 1 teaspoon dried thyme
2 teaspoons minced fresh or dried rosemary
$1/2$ teaspoon pepper
8 hamburger buns
Toppings: honey mustard, mayonnaise, lettuce, tomato slices

COMBINE 2 pounds ground turkey and next 5 ingredients, and shape into 8 patties.

GRILL patties, covered with grill lid, over medium-high heat (350° to 400°) 5 minutes on each side or until done. Serve on buns with desired toppings.

Mini-Cheeseburgers

Makes 20 burgers
Hands on: 20 min., Hands off: 17 min.

1 pound lean ground beef
2 tablespoons ketchup
$1/4$ teaspoon salt
$1/4$ teaspoon pepper
1 ($7^{1}/_2$-ounce) package party rolls
5 ($^3/_4$-ounce) American cheese slices, quartered
Toppings: mustard, ketchup, mayonnaise, minced onion, dill pickle slices, tomato slices, lettuce leaves

COMBINE beef and next 3 ingredients. Shape mixture by tablespoonfuls into patties, and place on a rack in a broiler pan.

BAKE at 350° for 15 to 17 minutes or until done.

SPLIT party rolls horizontally, and place a piece of cheese and a meat patty in each roll. Serve with desired toppings.

NOTE: Place cheeseburgers, without toppings, in zip-top plastic freezer bags; seal and freeze up to 1 month. Remove desired number of cheeseburgers from freezer, and thaw in refrigerator. Reheat cheeseburgers in microwave, if desired, and serve with desired toppings.

Greek Feta Burgers

Makes 4 servings
Hands on: 20 min.

THESE ARE DELICIOUS WITH OVEN-ROASTED POTATOES. SPRINKLE THE POTATOES WITH GREEK SEASONING FOR A COMPLEMENTARY FLAVOR.

1 pound ground chuck
1 (4-ounce) package crumbled feta cheese
1 garlic clove, minced
$1/4$ cup chopped fresh mint
1 teaspoon salt
$1/2$ teaspoon pepper
1 teaspoon chopped fresh or crushed dried rosemary
Fresh spinach leaves
4 hamburger buns with onions
2 plum tomatoes, chopped
1 small onion, diced
Cucumber-Dill Sauce

COMBINE first 7 ingredients; shape into 4 patties.

GRILL patties, covered with grill lid, over medium-high heat (350° to 400°) 5 minutes on each side or until done. Place patties on spinach-lined hamburger buns. Top with tomatoes, chopped onion, and Cucumber-Dill Sauce.

Cucumber-Dill Sauce:

Makes $1/2$ cup
Hands on: 5 min.

$1/4$ cup peeled, seeded, and diced cucumber
$1/4$ cup sour cream
$1/2$ teaspoon chopped fresh dill
1 garlic clove, minced

STIR together all ingredients. Cover and chill until ready to serve. ◆

Cucumber-Dill Sauce tops Greek Feta Burgers in onion buns.

Fuss-Free Wraps

For a quick meal, opt for these super simple sandwiches. They're easy to handle and portable enough to pack for school, work, or a leisurely picnic.

Choose pita bread rounds or whole grain or flavored tortillas—such as sun-dried tomato or spinach—and fill them with your favorite ingredients. Serve Fresh Pesto Pasta Salad to complete your menu.

Smoked Turkey Wraps and Fresh Pesto Pasta Salad are ideal for a bridal shower, ladies' luncheon, or most any midday gathering.

SMOKED TURKEY WRAPS

Makes 8 servings
Hands on: 15 min.

2 (6.5-ounce) packages garlic-and-herb spreadable cheese, softened
8 (10-inch) whole grain pita bread rounds or flour tortillas
Caramelized Onions
1½ pounds thinly sliced smoked turkey
16 bacon slices, cooked and crumbled
4 cups loosely packed arugula or gourmet mixed baby salad greens

SPREAD garlic-and-herb cheese evenly over each pita round; top evenly with Caramelized Onions, sliced smoked turkey, crumbled bacon, and arugula. Roll up pitas, and wrap in parchment paper; chill. Cut pitas in half to serve.
NOTE: For testing purposes only, we used Alouette Garlic et Herbes Gourmet Spreadable Cheese for garlic-and-herb spreadable cheese.

Caramelized Onions:
Makes 2 cups
Hands on: 25 min.

2 large sweet onions, diced
1 tablespoon sugar
2 tablespoons olive oil
2 teaspoons balsamic vinegar

COOK onions and 1 tablespoon sugar in hot oil in a skillet over medium-high heat, stirring often, 20 minutes or until onions are caramel colored. Stir in 2 teaspoons balsamic vinegar.

FRESH PESTO PASTA SALAD

Makes 8 servings
Hands on: 20 min.

1 (16-ounce) package small shell pasta
⅓ cup red wine vinegar
1 tablespoon sugar
1 teaspoon seasoned pepper
½ teaspoon salt
1 teaspoon Dijon mustard
1 garlic clove, pressed
¾ cup olive oil
1 cup chopped fresh basil
1 (3-ounce) package shredded Parmesan cheese
½ cup toasted pine nuts
Garnishes: gourmet mixed baby salad greens, grape tomatoes, yellow pear-shaped tomatoes

PREPARE pasta according to package directions; drain and chill.

WHISK together vinegar and next 5 ingredients. Gradually whisk in olive oil.

ADD vinaigrette to pasta. Add basil, cheese, and pine nuts; toss to combine. Garnish, if desired.

SOUTHWEST BLT WRAP

Makes 6 servings
Hands on: 30 min.

½ cup salsa
⅓ cup frozen corn, thawed
6 (8-inch) flour tortillas
18 bacon slices, cooked and
    crumbled
½ head iceberg lettuce, chopped
Avocado-Lime Sauce

STIR together ½ cup salsa and ⅓ cup corn.

TOP 1 side of each tortilla evenly with bacon, lettuce, and salsa mixture. Drizzle with Avocado-Lime Sauce. Roll up, and serve immediately.

Avocado-Lime Sauce:

Makes 1½ cups
Hands on: 5 min.

1 avocado, mashed
4 teaspoons fresh lime juice
½ cup mayonnaise
1 teaspoon chopped fresh cilantro
Salt to taste

STIR together all ingredients until thoroughly combined. Chill mixture until ready to serve.

TUNA CAESAR WRAPS

Makes 4 servings
Hands on: 20 min., Hands off: 2 hrs.

1 (6-ounce) can solid white tuna in
    water, drained and flaked
1 small red onion, thinly sliced and
    separated into rings
½ cup shredded carrot
½ medium-size green bell pepper, cut
    into strips
¼ cup Caesar dressing
4 (8-inch) flour tortillas
8 romaine lettuce leaves, torn
1 (2¼-ounce) can sliced black olives,
    drained
¼ cup grated Parmesan cheese

TOSS together first 5 ingredients; cover and chill 2 hours. Drain.

TOP tortillas evenly with lettuce leaves, tuna mixture, olives, and cheese. Roll up, and serve immediately. ◆

Enjoy a light Greek-style meal featuring Grilled Shrimp Gyros With Herbed Yogurt Spread. Dress them up with colorful corrugated paper tied with raffia.

GRILLED SHRIMP GYROS WITH HERBED YOGURT SPREAD

Makes 4 servings
Hands on: 30 min., Hands off: 30 min.

1½ pounds unpeeled, medium-size
    fresh shrimp
2 tablespoons Greek seasoning
2 tablespoons olive oil
6 (12-inch) wooden skewers
4 (8-inch) pita or gyro bread rounds
Herbed Yogurt Spread
½ cup crumbled feta cheese
1 large tomato, chopped
1 cucumber, thinly sliced

PEEL shrimp, and devein, if desired.

COMBINE Greek seasoning and olive oil in a zip-top plastic freezer bag; add shrimp. Seal and chill 30 minutes; drain.

SOAK skewers in water 30 minutes. Thread shrimp onto skewers.

GRILL shrimp skewers, covered with grill lid, over medium heat (300° to 350°) about 5 minutes on each side or just until shrimp turn pink.

WRAP each pita round in a damp cloth. Microwave at HIGH 10 to 15 seconds or until soft. Spread 1 side of each pita round with Herbed Yogurt Spread. Top evenly with shrimp, feta cheese, tomato, and cucumber. Roll up, and serve immediately.

Herbed Yogurt Spread:

Makes about ½ cup
Hands on: 5 min.

½ cup low-fat plain yogurt
1 garlic clove, minced
1 tablespoon chopped fresh or
    ¾ teaspoon dried oregano
1 teaspoon chopped fresh mint
2 teaspoons lemon juice
¼ teaspoon pepper

WHISK together ½ cup yogurt and remaining ingredients. Chill until ready to serve.

packaging tips

■ Line baskets or glazed flowerpots with decorative dinner napkins, and use as serving pieces.

■ Enhance containers with dried flowers and other decorative items secured with a glue gun.

Melt-in-Your-Mouth
Sandwiches

Strawberry jam, turkey, smoked ham, and melted
Swiss cheese rest atop seasoned French toast in
Open-Faced Monte Cristo Sandwiches.

These toasty sandwiches— grilled, broiled, or baked— are perfect for a no-fuss, casual supper. Pair any of them with a favorite soup or salad to complete your mouthwatering meal.

OPEN-FACED MONTE CRISTO SANDWICHES

Makes 4 servings
Hands on: 20 min.

2 large eggs
½ cup milk
½ teaspoon salt
¼ teaspoon pepper
4 (1-inch-thick) white bread slices
2 tablespoons butter or margarine
4 tablespoons strawberry jam or red currant jelly
4 ounces thinly sliced cooked turkey or chicken
4 ounces thinly sliced smoked cooked ham
8 (¾-ounce) Swiss cheese slices
Powdered sugar (optional)
Garnishes: sliced whole strawberries, whole strawberries

WHISK together first 4 ingredients in a shallow dish. Dip both sides of bread slices in egg mixture.

MELT butter in a large skillet over medium heat; add bread slices, and cook 2 to 3 minutes on each side or until golden brown.

SPREAD 1 tablespoon strawberry jam on 1 side of each bread slice; top evenly with turkey, smoked ham, and Swiss cheese slices. Place sandwiches on a baking sheet.

BROIL 5 inches from heat 2 to 3 minutes or until cheese melts. Sprinkle with powdered sugar, if desired. Garnish, if desired, and serve immediately.

GIANT MEATBALL SANDWICH

Makes 6 servings
Hands on: 25 min., Hands off: 10 min.

1 pound ground round
½ pound ground pork sausage
1 (28-ounce) jar spaghetti sauce with peppers and mushrooms
1 garlic clove, minced
1 (16-ounce) unsliced Italian bread loaf
1 (6-ounce) package sliced provolone cheese

COMBINE ground round and sausage; shape into 1-inch balls.

COOK meatballs in a large skillet over medium heat 10 to 15 minutes or until browned. Drain and return to skillet. Add spaghetti sauce and garlic; bring to a boil. Reduce heat, and simmer, stirring occasionally, 12 to 15 minutes or until meatballs are no longer pink in center.

CUT bread in half horizontally, and scoop out bottom, leaving a ½-inch-thick shell. Place bread shell and bread top, cut sides up, on a baking sheet. Broil 5½ inches from heat 1 to 2 minutes or until lightly toasted.

SPOON meatball mixture into toasted shell; top with provolone cheese slices. Cover with bread top. Cut sandwich into 6 pieces, and serve immediately.

OPEN-FACED CRAB MELTS

Makes 6 servings
Hands on: 10 min.

THIS SANDWICH WOULD ALSO BE A GREAT ADDITION TO A BRUNCH MENU.

1 pound fresh lump crabmeat, picked and drained*
¼ to ⅓ cup mayonnaise
½ teaspoon salt
¼ teaspoon pepper
¼ teaspoon sugar
3 English muffins, split and toasted
1 cup (4 ounces) shredded sharp Cheddar cheese

STIR together first 5 ingredients. Spread mixture evenly over cut sides of muffin halves; sprinkle evenly with cheese.

BROIL 5 inches from heat 2 to 3 minutes or until cheese is melted. Serve immediately.

*2 (6-ounce) cans lump crabmeat or 2 (6-ounce) cans solid white tuna in spring water, drained, may be substituted. ◆

ASPARAGUS HOT BROWNS

Makes 4 servings
Hands on: 20 min., Hands off: 30 min.

TO SAVE TIME, COOK THE BACON WHILE THE BREAD IS TOASTING.

1 pound fresh asparagus
1 (2-pound) deli roasted whole chicken
4 (1½-inch-thick) French bread slices
4 plum tomatoes, cut into ¼-inch-thick slices
½ teaspoon freshly ground pepper
1 (10-ounce) container refrigerated Alfredo sauce
½ cup (2 ounces) shredded Cheddar cheese
6 bacon slices, cooked and crumbled

SNAP off tough ends of asparagus, and remove scales with a vegetable peeler, if desired. Cook in boiling water to cover 1 minute or until crisp-tender; drain. Plunge asparagus into ice water to stop the cooking process; drain and set aside.

SKIN and bone chicken, cutting meat into bite-size pieces. Set aside.

PLACE bread slices on a baking sheet. Bake at 400° for 8 to 10 minutes or until lightly browned. Remove from oven.

ARRANGE bread in a lightly greased 11- x 7-inch baking dish. Place tomato slices evenly over bread. Sprinkle evenly with ½ teaspoon pepper. Top evenly with chicken and asparagus. Spoon Alfredo sauce evenly over asparagus. Sprinkle with ½ cup shredded Cheddar cheese.

BAKE at 400° for 15 to 20 minutes or until thoroughly heated. Sprinkle with cooked bacon.

For a fresh twist on a time-honored Louisville specialty, try smothered Asparagus Hot Browns.

Outdoor Celebration

Whether you're a beginner cook or a savvy host, this party menu is doable, easy, and perfect for any outdoor gathering. Pair these crowd-pleasing recipes with some of your traditional favorites. Short ingredient lists, make-ahead tips, and simple techniques make planning a breeze, giving you time to stop and smell the hydrangeas.

SPICY JACK CHEESE CRISPS

Makes 8 dozen
Hands on: 20 min.; Hands off: 8 hrs., 40 min.

½ cup butter, softened
2 (8-ounce) blocks Monterey Jack
   cheese with peppers, shredded
2 cups all-purpose flour
96 pecan halves

BEAT softened butter and Monterey Jack cheese at medium speed with an electric mixer until blended; add flour, beating until blended.
DIVIDE dough into 3 equal portions; shape each portion into a 6-inch log. Cover and chill at least 8 hours.
CUT each log into 32 (⅛-inch) slices, and place on ungreased baking sheets. Gently press 1 pecan half into center of each wafer.
BAKE, in batches, at 350° for 8 to 10 minutes. Remove crisps to wire racks to cool. Store in an airtight container. ▶

Garden Party

menu
(serves 10 to 12)

Chilled Shrimp With
Rémoulade Sauce
Balsamic Marinated Olives
Spicy Jack Cheese Crisps
crusty bread
Lemon Flank Steak Skewers
Mint Bellinis
Creamy Citrus Tartlets

Chilled Shrimp With Rémoulade Sauce, Lemon Flank Steak Skewers and Lemon Dipping Sauce, Balsamic Marinated Olives

CHILLED SHRIMP WITH RÉMOULADE SAUCE

Makes 10 to 12 appetizer servings
Hands on: 30 min.

IN A HURRY? SUBSTITUTE 2 (2-POUND) PACKAGES FROZEN, COOKED, PEELED, AND DEVEINED LARGE SHRIMP FOR FRESH SHRIMP. YOU CAN FIND THESE AT LARGE SUPERMARKETS.

4 pounds unpeeled, large fresh
   shrimp, cooked
Rémoulade Sauce
Lemon wedges

PEEL shrimp, and devein, if desired. Chill.
SERVE shrimp with Rémoulade Sauce and lemon wedges.

Rémoulade Sauce:
Makes 1 cup
Hands on: 10 min., Hands off: 1 hr.

¾ cup light mayonnaise
2 tablespoons chopped fresh
   parsley
2 tablespoons Creole mustard
1 tablespoon lemon juice
1 garlic clove, pressed
1 teaspoon paprika
¼ teaspoon salt

COMBINE all ingredients; cover and chill at least 1 hour.

Balsamic Marinated Olives

Makes 6 cups
Hands on: 15 min.; Hands off: 8 hrs., 30 min.

THIS MAKE-AHEAD RECIPE CAN BE EASILY HALVED.

2 (8-ounce) jars black olives, drained
2 (7-ounce) jars kalamata olives, drained
2 (7-ounce) jars pimiento-stuffed olives, drained
½ cup olive oil
½ cup balsamic vinegar
1 tablespoon Italian seasoning

COMBINE all ingredients; cover and chill at least 8 hours.

LET stand 30 minutes at room temperature before serving. Serve with a slotted spoon, or drain.

Thin lemon slices float atop Mint Bellinis in decorative stemware.

Mint Bellinis

Makes 9½ cups
Hands on: 10 min., Hands off: 20 min.

THESE REFRESHING SIPPERS LIVEN UP ANY PARTY.

4 (12-ounce) cans peach nectar
2 cups sugar
1 lemon, halved
¼ cup firmly packed fresh mint leaves
1 (750-milliliter) bottle Champagne or sparkling wine*
Garnish: lemon slices

BRING first 4 ingredients to a boil, and cook 20 minutes; cool.

REMOVE and discard lemon and mint; store mixture in an airtight container in refrigerator until ready to serve.

STIR in Champagne just before serving. Serve over ice; garnish, if desired.
*2½ cups sparkling water may be substituted.

CREAMY CITRUS TARTLETS

Makes 30 tartlets
Hands on: 25 min.; Hands off: 1 hr., 20 min.

LOOK FOR ORANGE AND LEMON CURD ON THE GROCERY AISLE WITH THE JAMS AND JELLIES.

2 (2.1-ounce) packages frozen mini phyllo pastry shells
1 cup whipping cream, divided
⅓ cup orange curd
½ teaspoon almond extract, divided
⅓ cup lemon curd

BAKE pastry shells according to package directions; cool completely.

BEAT ½ cup whipping cream, ⅓ cup orange curd, and ¼ teaspoon almond extract at medium speed with an electric mixer until thickened and soft peaks form. Spoon the mixture evenly into half of pastry shells.

BEAT lemon curd, remaining ½ cup cream, and remaining ¼ teaspoon extract at medium speed with an electric mixer until thickened and soft peaks form. Spoon into remaining shells.

CHILL tartlets 1 hour.

NOTE: For testing purposes only, we used Dickinson's Orange Curd and Lemon Curd.

LEMON FLANK STEAK SKEWERS

Makes 12 to 16 appetizer servings
Hands on: 40 min., Hands off: 8 hrs.

FOR EASY SLICING, FREEZE MEAT FOR 10 MINUTES FIRST.

⅔ cup olive oil
4 teaspoons grated lemon rind
½ cup fresh lemon juice
2 teaspoons salt
½ teaspoon dried crushed red pepper
4 (2-pound) flank steaks, cut diagonally into ¼-inch slices
50 (12-inch) wooden skewers
Lemon Dipping Sauce
Garnish: flat-leaf parsley

COMBINE first 5 ingredients in a shallow dish or zip-top plastic freezer bag; add steak. Cover or seal, and chill 8 hours, turning occasionally.

SOAK skewers in water 30 minutes.

REMOVE steak from marinade, discarding marinade.

THREAD each steak slice onto 1 skewer.

GRILL skewers, covered with grill lid, over medium-high heat (350° to 400°) 4 to 5 minutes on each side or to desired degree of doneness. Serve with Lemon Dipping Sauce. Garnish, if desired.

Horseradish adds a kick to the dipping sauce for Lemon Flank Steak Skewers.

Lemon Dipping Sauce:

Makes 4½ cups
Hands on: 15 min., Hands off: 1 hr.

ONE MEDIUM LEMON YIELDS 2 TO 3 TABLESPOONS LEMON JUICE AND ABOUT 2 TEASPOONS LEMON ZEST. USE A ZESTER TO GRATE THE RIND.

2 (16-ounce) containers light sour cream
2 tablespoons prepared horseradish
2 teaspoons grated lemon rind
6 tablespoons fresh lemon juice
1 teaspoon salt

COMBINE all ingredients; cover and chill at least 1 hour. ◆

planning makes perfect

Two Weeks Ahead
■ Prepare and freeze dough logs for Spicy Jack Cheese Crisps.
■ Make and refrigerate Balsamic Marinated Olives.

Three Days Ahead
■ Shop for perishable items, pantry staples, and beverages.
■ Order fresh shrimp.
■ Prepare and refrigerate peach nectar mixture for Mint Bellinis, omitting Champagne or sparkling water.
■ Thaw dough logs in the refrigerator, and bake Spicy Jack Cheese Crisps as directed. Store in an airtight container at room temperature.

One to Two Days Ahead
■ Prepare and chill Lemon Dipping Sauce and Rémoulade Sauce.
■ Purchase extra bags of ice for shrimp and Mint Bellinis. (Ask a neighbor to help with storage, if necessary.)

One Day Ahead
■ Cook shrimp. Store in a large zip-top plastic freezer bag, and place over a pan of ice in refrigerator.
■ Slice lemons for garnishes (crosswise slices for Mint Bellinis, wedges for shrimp). Wrap in a damp paper towel, and store in a zip-top plastic bag in refrigerator.
■ Bake pastry shells for Creamy Citrus Tartlets. Store in an airtight container or tin at room temperature.
■ Marinate Lemon Flank Steak Skewers overnight in refrigerator.
■ Chill bottles of Champagne or sparkling wine for Mint Bellinis.

Party Day
■ Make tartlet filling, assemble tartlets, and chill.
■ Let Balsamic Marinated Olives stand at room temperature 30 minutes; drain, if desired. Spoon mixture into a serving bowl.
■ Slice breads to accompany dishes.
■ Soak skewers, and grill flank steak just before guests arrive.

Come by for Brunch

Brie-and-Sausage Brunch Casserole,
Spiced Apples, Pecan Crescent Twists,
and Mulled Cranberry Drink are
a delectable way to start to the day.

Entice family and friends with a combination of sweet and savory dishes. Pair any of these baked egg dishes with a breakfast bread, fresh fruit, and warm beverage. Guests will be glad they came.

PECAN CRESCENT TWISTS

Makes 8 servings
Hands on: 20 min., Hands off: 10 min.

2 (8-ounce) cans refrigerated crescent rolls
3 tablespoons butter or margarine, melted and divided
1/2 cup chopped pecans
1/4 cup granulated sugar
1 teaspoon ground cinnamon
1/8 teaspoon ground nutmeg
1/2 cup powdered sugar
2 1/2 teaspoons maple syrup or milk

UNROLL crescent rolls, and separate each can into 2 rectangles, pressing perforations to seal. Brush evenly with 2 tablespoons melted butter.
STIR together chopped pecans and next 3 ingredients; sprinkle 3 tablespoons pecan mixture onto buttered side of each rectangle, pressing in gently.
ROLL up, starting at one long side, and twist. Cut 6 shallow 1/2-inch-long diagonal slits in each roll.

SHAPE rolls into rings, pressing ends together; place on a lightly greased baking sheet. Brush rings evenly with remaining 1 tablespoon butter.
BAKE at 375° for 12 minutes or until rings are golden.
STIR together powdered sugar and maple syrup until glaze is smooth; drizzle evenly over warm rings. Cut rings in half, and serve.

SPICED APPLES

Makes 8 servings
Hands on: 35 min.

1/2 cup butter or margarine
8 large Granny Smith apples, peeled, cored, and sliced
1 1/2 cups sugar
1 1/2 teaspoons ground cinnamon
1/2 teaspoon ground nutmeg

MELT 1/2 cup butter in a large skillet over medium-high heat; add apples and remaining ingredients. Sauté 15 to 20 minutes or until apples are tender.

BRIE-AND-SAUSAGE BRUNCH CASSEROLE

Makes 8 to 10 servings
Hands on: 20 min., Hands off: 9 hrs.

1 (8-ounce) round Brie*
1 pound ground hot pork sausage
6 white sandwich bread slices
1 cup grated Parmesan cheese
7 large eggs, divided
3 cups whipping cream, divided
2 cups milk
1 tablespoon chopped fresh sage or
    1 teaspoon dried rubbed sage
1 teaspoon seasoned salt
1 teaspoon dry mustard
Garnishes: chopped green onions, shaved Parmesan cheese

TRIM rind from Brie, and discard; cut cheese into cubes, and set aside.
COOK ground pork sausage in a large skillet over medium-high heat, stirring until it crumbles and is no longer pink; drain well.

CUT crusts from bread slices, and place crusts evenly in bottom of a lightly greased 13- x 9-inch baking dish. Layer evenly with bread slices, sausage, and Brie; sprinkle with 1 cup grated Parmesan cheese.
WHISK together 5 eggs, 2 cups whipping cream, and next 4 ingredients; pour evenly over Brie and Parmesan cheeses in baking dish. Cover and chill 8 hours.
WHISK together remaining 2 eggs and remaining 1 cup whipping cream; pour evenly over chilled mixture.
BAKE, uncovered, at 350° for 1 hour or until casserole is set. Garnish, if desired.
*2 cups (8 ounces) shredded Swiss cheese may be substituted for 1 (8-ounce) round Brie.

MULLED CRANBERRY DRINK

Makes about 12 cups
Hands on: 10 min.

1 (48-ounce) bottle cranberry juice drink
3 cups apple juice
3 cups orange juice
1/2 cup maple syrup
1 1/2 teaspoons ground cinnamon
3/4 teaspoon ground cloves
3/4 teaspoon ground nutmeg
1 orange, sliced

BRING first 7 ingredients to a boil in a Dutch oven; reduce heat to low, and keep warm until ready to serve. Add orange slices just before serving.

GRANOLA

Makes 10 cups
Hands on: 15 min.; Hands off: 1 hr., 45 min.
SERVE WITH YOGURT AND FRESH FRUIT.

4 cups uncooked regular oats
1 cup sunflower seeds
1/2 cup whole almonds
1/2 cup sesame seeds
3/4 cup wheat germ
1 (3.5-ounce) can sweetened flaked coconut
1/2 cup honey
1/3 cup vegetable oil
2 tablespoons water
1 cup dried apricots, coarsely chopped
1 cup raisins

COMBINE first 6 ingredients in a large bowl. Stir together honey, oil, and water. Pour over oat mixture; toss well. Spread mixture into a lightly greased 15- x 10-inch jelly-roll pan.
BAKE at 225° for 1 hour and 45 minutes, stirring occasionally.
STIR in apricots and raisins. Cool completely. Store in an airtight container.

CAFÉ MOCHA LATTE

Makes 4 cups
Hands on: 10 min.

1 1/2 cups half-and-half
2 tablespoons brown sugar
2 cups strong brewed coffee or espresso
1/4 cup chocolate syrup
1 teaspoon vanilla extract
1/4 cup bourbon (optional)

HEAT half-and-half in a saucepan over medium-high heat. (Do not boil.) Remove from heat; stir in brown sugar, next 3 ingredients, and, if desired, bourbon. Serve warm or over ice. ▶

BACON BISCUIT CUPS

Makes 10 servings
Hands on: 15 min., Hands off: 22 min.

2 (3-ounce) packages cream cheese, softened
2 tablespoons milk
1 large egg
½ cup (2 ounces) shredded Swiss cheese
1 green onion, chopped
1 (10-ounce) can refrigerated biscuits
5 bacon slices, cooked and crumbled

BEAT first 3 ingredients at medium speed with an electric mixer until blended. Stir in cheese and green onion.

SEPARATE biscuits into 10 portions. Pat each portion into a 5-inch circle, and press on bottom and up sides of greased muffin cups, forming a ¼-inch edge. Sprinkle evenly with half of cooked bacon, and spoon cream cheese mixture evenly on top.

BAKE at 375° for 22 minutes or until set. Sprinkle with remaining bacon, lightly pressing into filling. Remove immediately from pan, and serve warm.

CREAMY HASH BROWN CASSEROLE

Makes 6 servings
Hands on: 10 min.; Hands off: 1 hr., 10 min.

THIS LIGHTENED VERSION TASTES JUST AS RICH AS THE TRADITIONAL BUT HAS LESS SATURATED FAT AND CALORIES.

1 (32-ounce) package frozen hash brown potatoes
1 (10¾-ounce) can fat-free cream of chicken soup
1 (8-ounce) container light sour cream
1 small onion, chopped
1 (5-ounce) can low-fat evaporated milk
¼ cup light butter or margarine, melted
1 teaspoon dried rosemary (optional)
½ teaspoon salt
¼ teaspoon pepper
1 cup (4 ounces) shredded reduced-fat Cheddar cheese

STIR together potatoes and next 8 ingredients in a large bowl.

SPOON mixture into a lightly greased 11- x 7-inch baking dish. Sprinkle cheese evenly over top.

BAKE at 350° for 1 hour or until bubbly and golden. Remove from oven, and let stand 10 minutes.

Serve Bacon Biscuit Cups fresh from the oven with a hot cup of coffee.

QUICHE LORRAINE

Makes 6 servings
Hands on: 20 min., Hands off: 1 hr.

BAKING THE QUICHE ON THE LOWEST OVEN RACK YIELDS A CRISPIER CRUST.

½ (15-ounce) package refrigerated piecrusts
8 bacon slices, chopped
4 green onions, chopped
2 cups (8 ounces) shredded Swiss cheese, divided
6 large eggs
1 cup whipping cream
1 tablespoon Dijon mustard
½ teaspoon salt
⅛ teaspoon ground nutmeg
⅛ teaspoon ground red pepper

FIT 1 piecrust into a 9-inch deep-dish pieplate according to package directions; fold edges under, and crimp.

BAKE piecrust on lowest oven rack at 400° for 8 minutes; cool.

COOK bacon in a skillet over medium-high heat until crisp; add green onions, and sauté 1 minute. Drain well. Spoon bacon mixture into piecrust. Sprinkle with 1 cup shredded Swiss cheese.

WHISK together eggs and next 5 ingredients. Pour egg mixture into piecrust, and sprinkle with remaining 1 cup shredded Swiss cheese.

BAKE on lowest oven rack at 400° for 35 minutes or until set. Let stand 10 minutes before serving.

EGGPLANT-AND-ROASTED PEPPER FRITTATA

Makes 6 servings
Hands on: 20 min., Hands off: 10 min.

6 large eggs
1/2 cup milk
1 teaspoon dried oregano
1/2 teaspoon salt
1/4 teaspoon pepper
1/2 cup shredded Parmesan cheese, divided
1 medium eggplant, peeled and chopped (2 cups)
1 garlic clove, minced
1 tablespoon olive oil
1 (7-ounce) jar roasted red bell peppers, drained and chopped

WHISK together first 5 ingredients until blended. Stir in 1/4 cup Parmesan cheese. Set aside.

SAUTÉ eggplant and garlic in hot oil in a 10-inch ovenproof nonstick skillet over medium-high heat 2 to 3 minutes or until tender. Stir in roasted peppers.

ADD egg mixture to skillet. As it starts to cook, lift edges with a spatula, and tilt pan so uncooked portion flows underneath.

BAKE at 400° for 7 minutes or until set. Sprinkle with remaining 1/4 cup cheese. Let stand 3 minutes. Cut into wedges, and serve immediately.

BREAKFAST BURRITOS

Makes 5 servings
Hands on: 30 min.

5 (12-inch) flour tortillas
1 1/2 cups frozen hash browns, thawed
3 tablespoons vegetable oil
1 small green bell pepper, chopped
1 small red bell pepper, chopped
6 large eggs, lightly beaten
1/4 cup chopped fresh cilantro
1/2 teaspoon salt
1/4 teaspoon pepper
Toppings: salsa, sour cream

HEAT tortillas according to package directions; keep warm.

SAUTÉ hash browns in hot oil in a large skillet 6 to 8 minutes; add bell peppers, and sauté 5 minutes or until tender. Add eggs, and cook, stirring occasionally, 3 minutes or until eggs are done. Stir in cilantro, salt, and pepper.

SPOON egg mixture evenly down centers of tortillas; roll up. Wrap individually in wax paper or aluminum foil. Serve with desired toppings. ◆

dress up your gathering

Here are some simple ways to embellish your brunch buffet.

■ Layer inexpensive sheer fabric over a solid tablecloth to add depth and interest to the table.

■ Create different heights by using cake stands to display breads and fruits. Or position less attractive items, such as books or small boxes, underneath fabric to create an elevated surface.

■ For simple centerpieces, arrange colorful fruit or tall candles in oversize glass vases.

■ To give your gathering a more formal touch, serve orange juice with sparkling wine in crystal goblets or Champagne flutes.

■ Add eye-pleasing garnishes, such as fresh herb sprigs, citrus rind curls, or a sprinkle of seasoning, to each brunch plate.

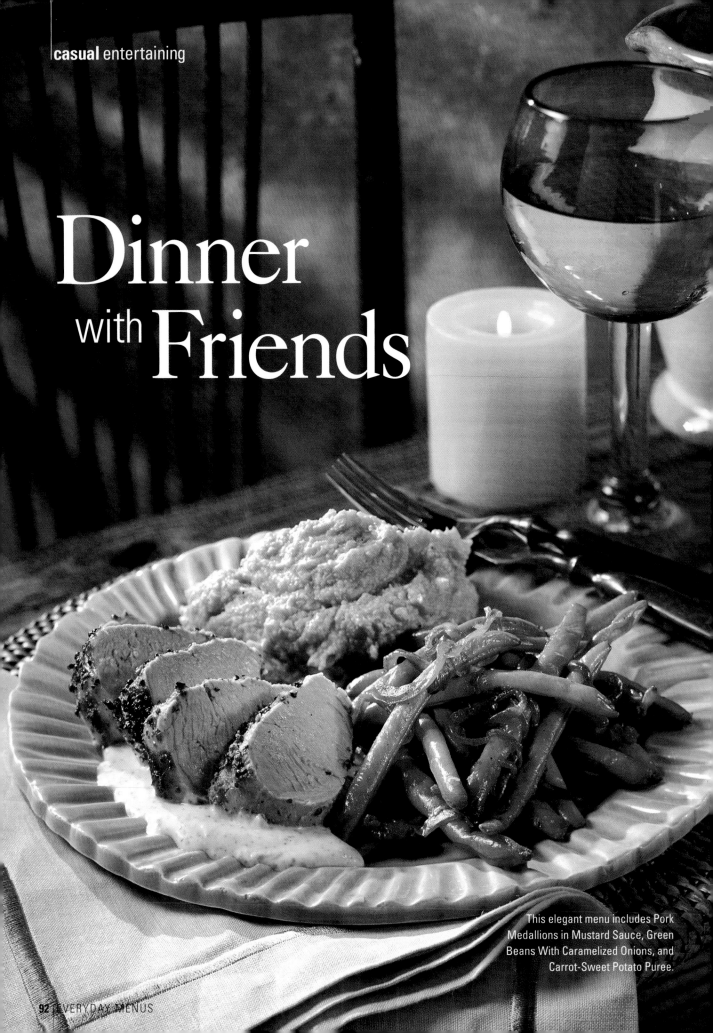

Dinner with Friends

This elegant menu includes Pork Medallions in Mustard Sauce, Green Beans With Caramelized Onions, and Carrot-Sweet Potato Puree.

Invite another couple over for a cozy meal with this scrumptious dinner-party menu, perfect for a cold-weather gathering. Or double these recipes for your next supper club get-together. Not sure which wines to choose? Pork dishes offer flexibility in wine selection. Follow the countdown guide and wine-pairing tips on page 95 for easy planning.

PORK MEDALLIONS IN MUSTARD SAUCE

Makes 4 servings
Hands on: 10 min.; Hands off: 8 hrs., 30 min.
2 tablespoons vegetable oil
2 tablespoons coarse-grained mustard
½ teaspoon salt
½ teaspoon coarsely ground pepper
1½ pounds pork tenderloin
¼ cup dry white wine or chicken broth
Mustard Sauce

STIR together first 4 ingredients. Rub mixture over pork, and place in a large zip-top plastic freezer bag. Seal and chill 8 hours. Place pork on a lightly greased rack in a shallow roasting pan.
BAKE at 450° for 15 minutes. Reduce temperature to 400°, and bake 15 minutes or until a meat thermometer inserted into thickest portion registers 160°, basting with wine after 10 minutes. Slice and serve with Mustard Sauce.

Easy-Does-It Dinner

menu
(serves 4 or double to serve 8)

Warmed Cranberry Brie

Citrusy Pecans

Pork Medallions in Mustard Sauce

Carrot-Sweet Potato Puree

Green Beans With Caramelized Onions

Sour Cream Yeast Rolls

Grown-up Hot Chocolate

Pecan Toffee

Mustard Sauce:
Makes about 1½ cups
Hands on: 25 min.
1¾ cups whipping cream
¼ cup coarse-grain mustard
¼ teaspoon salt
⅛ teaspoon ground white pepper

COOK cream in a heavy saucepan over medium heat 20 minutes or until reduced to 1¼ cups. (Do not boil.) Stir in remaining ingredients, and cook 1 minute.

CARROT-SWEET POTATO PUREE

Makes 6 servings
Hands on: 20 min., Hands off: 17 min.
THIS RECIPE REQUIRES NO STOVE-TOP COOKING; IT'S ALL DONE IN THE MICROWAVE. WE REDUCED CALORIES, FAT, AND CHOLESTEROL BY USING LIGHT BUTTER (AND LESS OF IT) AND LIGHT SOUR CREAM.

5 carrots, sliced
¾ cup water
¼ cup light butter or margarine
1 (29-ounce) can sweet potatoes, drained
1 (16-ounce) can sweet potatoes, drained
1 (8-ounce) container light sour cream
1 tablespoon sugar
1 teaspoon grated lemon rind
½ teaspoon ground nutmeg
¼ teaspoon salt
¼ teaspoon ground black pepper
⅛ teaspoon ground red pepper

MICROWAVE carrots and ¾ cup water in a glass bowl at HIGH 8 to 12 minutes or until tender. Drain.
PROCESS carrots and butter in a food processor until mixture is smooth, stopping to scrape down sides. Add sweet potatoes; process until smooth.
STIR together sweet potato mixture, sour cream, and remaining ingredients.

SPOON mixture into a 1½-quart glass dish. Microwave at HIGH 4 to 5 minutes or until thoroughly heated.
NOTE: To make ahead, prepare and stir together ingredients as directed; cover and chill up to 2 days. Let stand at room temperature 30 minutes; microwave as directed.

SOUR CREAM YEAST ROLLS

Makes 1 dozen
Hands on: 30 min.; Hands off: 9 hrs., 12 min.
1 (¼-ounce) envelope active dry yeast
¼ cup warm water (100° to 110°)
½ cup sour cream
¼ cup butter or margarine
¼ cup sugar
½ teaspoon salt
1 large egg, lightly beaten
2 cups all-purpose flour
Melted butter

DISSOLVE yeast in ¼ cup warm water in a large mixing bowl; let stand 5 minutes.
COOK ½ cup sour cream and next 3 ingredients in a saucepan over low heat, stirring occasionally, until butter melts. Cool to 100° to 110°.
STIR sour cream mixture and egg into yeast mixture. Gradually add 2 cups flour, mixing well. (Dough will be wet.) Cover and chill 8 hours.
PUNCH dough down. Shape into 36 (1-inch) balls; place 3 balls in each cup of a lightly greased muffin pan. Cover and let rise in a warm place (85°), free from drafts, 1 hour or until doubled in bulk.
BAKE at 375° for 10 to 12 minutes or until golden brown. Brush rolls with melted butter.
NOTE: Freeze baked rolls up to 1 month, if desired. To reheat, wrap frozen rolls in aluminum foil, and bake at 400° for 15 minutes or until thoroughly heated. ▶

For dessert, sip Grown-up Hot Chocolate, and nibble rich **Pecan Toffee**.

wine pairings

White wines: Viognier, Joseph Phelps; Riesling, Hogue; Chardonnay, "Russian River Ranches," Sonoma-Cutrer
Red wines: Pinot Noir, Rex Hill; Pinot Noir, Bridgeview Vineyard; Pinot Noir, Firesteed

GROWN-UP HOT CHOCOLATE

Makes 5 cups
Hands on: 10 min.

¼ cup boiling water
⅓ cup chocolate syrup
4 cups milk
⅓ to ½ cup coffee liqueur
Garnish: whipped cream

STIR together ¼ cup boiling water and chocolate syrup in a medium saucepan; add milk, stirring until blended. Cook over medium heat 6 to 8 minutes or until thoroughly heated. Stir in desired amount of coffee liqueur. Garnish, if desired.
NOTE: For testing purposes only, we used Kahlúa for coffee liqueur.

PECAN TOFFEE

Makes 1¾ pounds
Hands on: 25 min., Hands off: 30 min.

1½ cups chopped pecans, divided
1 cup sugar
1 cup butter, softened
⅓ cup water
5 (1.55-ounce) milk chocolate bars, broken into small pieces

LINE a 15- x 10-inch jelly-roll pan with heavy-duty aluminum foil; lightly grease foil. Sprinkle with 1 cup pecans to within 1 inch of edges.
BRING sugar, butter, and ⅓ cup water to a boil in a heavy saucepan over medium heat, stirring constantly. Cook over medium-high heat, stirring constantly, 12 minutes or until a candy thermometer registers 310° (hard-crack stage). Pour over pecans; sprinkle with chocolate pieces. Let stand 30 seconds.
SPRINKLE with remaining ½ cup pecans. Chill 30 minutes. Break up toffee using a mallet or rolling pin. Store in an airtight container up to 1 week.

GREEN BEANS WITH CARAMELIZED ONIONS

Makes 4 servings
Hands on: 35 min., Hands off: 10 min.

1 pound fresh green beans, trimmed
2 medium-size sweet onions, halved and thinly sliced
2 tablespoons butter or margarine
2 tablespoons brown sugar
1 to 2 teaspoons balsamic vinegar (optional)

COOK green beans in boiling water to cover 15 minutes; plunge into ice water to stop the cooking process, and drain. Chill 8 hours, if desired.
COOK onions in a large nonstick skillet over medium-high heat 8 to 10 minutes. (Do not stir.) Cook, stirring often, 5 to 10 minutes or until golden brown. Reduce heat to medium; stir in butter and brown sugar. Add green beans; cook 5 minutes or until thoroughly heated. Toss with vinegar, if desired.

WARMED CRANBERRY BRIE

Makes 8 appetizer servings
Hands on: 15 min., Hands off: 5 min.

THIS ALMOST-EFFORTLESS APPETIZER IS READY IN JUST MINUTES.

1 (15-ounce) round Brie
1 (16-ounce) can whole-berry cranberry sauce
¼ cup firmly packed brown sugar
2 tablespoons spiced rum*
½ teaspoon ground nutmeg
¼ cup chopped pecans, toasted
Apple and pear slices

TRIM rind from top of Brie, leaving a ⅓-inch border. Place on a baking sheet.
STIR together cranberry sauce and next 3 ingredients; spread mixture evenly over top of Brie. Sprinkle with pecans.
BAKE Brie at 500° for 5 minutes. Serve with apple and pear slices.
*2 tablespoons orange juice may be substituted for spiced rum.

CITRUSY PECANS

Makes 2 cups
Hands on: 15 min., Hands off: 25 min.

THESE SWEET, CRUNCHY NUTS ARE GREAT BY THE HANDFUL, OR YOU CAN ALSO CHOP THEM AND ADD TO SALADS AND SPREADS. BE SURE TO STORE THE PECANS IN AN AIRTIGHT CONTAINER OR A SEALED ZIP-TOP PLASTIC BAG TO PREVENT THEM FROM BECOMING STICKY.

1 egg white
2 cups pecan halves
½ cup firmly packed light brown sugar
2 teaspoons grated orange rind
2 tablespoons fresh orange juice
½ teaspoon salt
¼ teaspoon ground cinnamon
Vegetable cooking spray

WHISK egg white in a medium bowl until frothy; toss with pecans.
STIR together ½ cup brown sugar and next 4 ingredients in a large bowl. Add pecans, and toss. Drain well. Place pecans in a single layer on an aluminum foil-lined baking sheet coated with cooking spray.
BAKE at 325°, stirring occasionally, for 20 to 25 minutes. ◆

countdown to dinner

- Up to 1 month ahead: Prepare, bake, and freeze Sour Cream Yeast Rolls.
- Up to 1 week ahead: Make Pecan Toffee.
- One day ahead: Prepare Carrot-Sweet Potato Puree, and cook the green beans; refrigerate.
- 35 minutes: Remove puree from refrigerator. Let stand at room temperature.
- 30 minutes: Place pork tenderloins in preheated oven to bake. Begin preparing Mustard Sauce while pork bakes and onions caramelize.
- 15 minutes: Remove Sour Cream Yeast Rolls from freezer, wrap in aluminum foil, and place in oven with pork tenderloins.
- 10 minutes: Prepare Grown-up Hot Chocolate.
- 5 minutes: Add cooked green beans to onions, and cook until thoroughly heated; microwave puree.

Vegetable Sides Made Simple

If you're wondering what to serve with dinner tonight, then you've turned to the right page. Round out your meal with any of these veggie dishes, including fresh tomato recipes, quick sautés, and savory salads. Read on for heartier sides (page 102) and breads (page 104).

MEXICAN-STYLE CORN

Makes 4 servings
Hands on: 30 min.

SALSA VERDE IS A GREEN SAUCE TYPICALLY MADE FROM TOMATILLOS, GREEN CHILES, AND CILANTRO. LOOK FOR IT IN THE ETHNIC FOOD SECTION OF YOUR GROCERY STORE.

1 small onion, diced
1 small green bell pepper, diced
1 small red bell pepper, diced
1 teaspoon minced garlic
1 tablespoon canola oil
1 (16-ounce) package frozen whole kernel corn, thawed
1/4 cup salsa verde
1 teaspoon salt
1/2 teaspoon pepper
1/4 teaspoon ground cumin
1 medium tomato, peeled, seeded, and diced
1 tablespoon chopped fresh cilantro
Garnish: fresh cilantro sprigs

SAUTÉ first 4 ingredients in hot oil in a large skillet over medium heat 3 minutes;

left: Make a meal out of Honey-Tarragon Glazed Baby Carrots, Mexican-Style Corn, and Greens Beans Balsamic With Garlic.

add corn, and sauté 3 minutes.
STIR in salsa verde and next 3 ingredients, and cook 1 minute. Stir in diced tomato and chopped cilantro; cook 2 minutes or until thoroughly heated. Garnish, if desired.

GREEN BEANS BALSAMIC WITH GARLIC

Makes 4 servings
Hands on: 20 min., Hands off: 6 min.

FOR ADDED FLAVOR, STIR IN TOASTED CHOPPED WALNUTS OR PECANS.

2 pounds fresh green beans, trimmed
1 garlic clove, minced
2 tablespoons olive oil
2 tablespoons balsamic vinegar
1/4 teaspoon salt
1/4 teaspoon pepper

COOK green beans in boiling salted water to cover 6 minutes; drain. Plunge beans into ice water to stop the cooking process; drain.
SAUTÉ garlic in hot oil in a large skillet over medium-high heat 1 minute; add green beans, and sauté 3 to 4 minutes. Add balsamic vinegar, salt, and pepper; sauté 1 minute.

HONEY-TARRAGON GLAZED BABY CARROTS

Makes 6 servings
Hands on: 10 min., Hands off: 10 min.

SUBSTITUTE ANOTHER HERB, SUCH AS DILL OR BASIL, FOR TARRAGON IF YOU PREFER.

1 (2-pound) package peeled baby carrots
1 teaspoon lemon juice
1/2 teaspoon salt, divided
1/4 cup butter or margarine
1/4 cup honey
2 tablespoons chopped fresh tarragon or 2 teaspoons dried tarragon
1/4 teaspoon pepper
Garnish: fresh tarragon sprigs

COOK baby carrots, 1 teaspoon lemon juice, and 1/4 teaspoon salt in boiling water to cover 8 to 10 minutes; drain. Plunge into ice water to stop the cooking process; drain.
HEAT butter and honey in a large saucepan over medium-high heat, stirring until butter melts. Stir in remaining 1/4 teaspoon salt, carrots, tarragon, and pepper; cook 2 minutes or until thoroughly heated. Garnish, if desired. ▶

Tomato Napoleon—stacked with layers of in-season tomatoes, fresh mozzarella, and shredded basil—is the ideal accompaniment for a summer menu.

TOMATO NAPOLEON

Makes 4 servings
Hands on: 20 min., Hands off: 1 hr.

8 ounces fresh mozzarella cheese, cut into 8 slices
¾ cup Fresh Tomato Dressing (see recipe on page 100)
3 large tomatoes, each cut into 4 slices
1 teaspoon salt
1 teaspoon pepper
24 fresh basil leaves, shredded

PLACE cheese in a shallow dish.
POUR Fresh Tomato Dressing over cheese; cover and chill 1 hour.
REMOVE cheese slices, reserving tomato dressing.
SPRINKLE tomato slices evenly with salt and pepper.
PLACE 1 tomato slice on each of 4 salad plates; top each with 1 cheese slice and 2 shredded basil leaves. Repeat procedure with 1 tomato slice, 1 cheese slice, and 2 shredded basil leaves. Top with remaining tomato slices and basil. Drizzle evenly with reserved dressing.

RATATOUILLE

Makes 6 servings
Hands on: 25 min., Hands off: 15 min.

1 eggplant
1 tablespoon salt
2 zucchini
1 green bell pepper
1 red bell pepper
6 tomatoes, peeled and seeded
1 small onion, diced
1 tablespoon minced garlic
2 tablespoons olive oil
½ cup dry red wine
1 tablespoon red wine vinegar
2 tablespoons thinly sliced fresh basil or 2 teaspoons dried basil
2 tablespoons chopped fresh parsley
1 teaspoon chopped fresh oregano or ¼ teaspoon dried oregano
1 teaspoon salt
½ teaspoon pepper

PEEL eggplant, and cut into ½-inch cubes; sprinkle evenly with 1 tablespoon salt. Place in colander; let stand 15 to 20 minutes. Rinse well, and pat dry; set aside.
CUT zucchini and next 3 ingredients into ½-inch cubes.
SAUTÉ onion and garlic in hot oil in a large saucepan over medium-high heat 2 to 3 minutes; add cubed vegetables, red wine, and vinegar. Cook over medium heat, stirring occasionally, 10 to 15 minutes or until vegetables are tender. Stir in basil and remaining ingredients.

FRIED GREEN TOMATOES

Makes 4 servings
Hands on: 25 min.

2 medium-size green tomatoes
1 tablespoon Dijon mustard
1 teaspoon sugar
½ teaspoon salt
¼ teaspoon paprika
⅛ teaspoon ground red pepper
1½ teaspoons Worcestershire sauce
½ cup yellow cornmeal
¼ cup hot bacon drippings

CUT green tomatoes into ¼-inch-thick slices; chill.
COMBINE 1 tablespoon Dijon mustard and next 5 ingredients; spread on both sides of tomato slices. Coat tomatoes with cornmeal.
FRY tomato slices in hot drippings in a skillet over medium heat 3 minutes on each side or until browned. Drain on paper towels.

CREAMED FRESH CORN

Makes 2 cups
Hands on: 20 min.

4 ears fresh corn
1 teaspoon sugar (optional)
¼ cup butter or margarine
⅓ cup whipping cream
¼ teaspoon salt
½ teaspoon pepper

REMOVE husks and silks from corn. Cut corn from cobs, scraping cobs over bowl to remove milk. Stir in sugar, if desired.
MELT butter in medium saucepan over medium heat; add corn, and sauté 1 minute. Gradually stir in whipping cream; cook, stirring often, 10 to 12 minutes or until liquid is absorbed. Stir in salt and pepper. Serve immediately.

OKRA FRITTERS

Makes 3 dozen
Hands on: 30 min.

¾ cup yellow cornmeal
¾ cup all-purpose flour
4 large eggs
½ cup salsa
1 tablespoon seasoned salt
2 cups chopped fresh okra (about 1 pound)

1 large tomato, seeded and diced
1/2 green bell pepper, chopped
1 small onion, chopped
6 green onions, chopped
1/2 teaspoon salt
1/4 teaspoon ground red pepper (optional)
Vegetable oil

STIR together first 5 ingredients in a large bowl; stir in okra, next 5 ingredients, and if desired, ground red pepper.
POUR oil to depth of 2 inches into a Dutch oven; heat to 375°. Drop batter by tablespoonfuls into hot oil, and fry in batches until golden, turning once. Drain on paper towels, and serve immediately.

ASPARAGUS WITH LEMON BUTTER

Makes 4 to 6 servings
Hands on: 20 min.

2 pounds fresh asparagus
1/4 cup butter or margarine
1/2 teaspoon salt
1/2 teaspoon freshly ground pepper
1 tablespoon grated lemon rind
1/4 cup fresh lemon juice

SNAP off tough ends of asparagus; remove scales with a vegetable peeler.
MELT butter in a skillet over medium-high heat; add asparagus, and sauté 3 minutes or until crisp-tender. Add salt and pepper; remove from heat. Toss with lemon rind and juice.

GREEK TOMATOES

Makes 6 servings
Hands on: 20 min.

YOU CAN ALSO SERVE THIS DISH AS A SALAD BY CHOPPING THE TOMATOES AND TOSSING TOGETHER ALL THE INGREDIENTS IN A BOWL.

4 medium tomatoes, cut into 1/4-inch-thick slices
1/4 cup capers, drained and rinsed
1 (4-ounce) package crumbled feta cheese
1/4 cup finely chopped fresh parsley
Coarsely ground pepper
2 tablespoons olive oil

PLACE tomatoes on a platter. Sprinkle with capers and next 3 ingredients; drizzle with oil.

CREAMY SWEET SLAW

Makes 8 servings
Hands on: 20 min.

1/2 cup sugar
1/4 cup white vinegar
3/4 cup mayonnaise
1/3 cup evaporated milk
1 teaspoon salt
1/2 teaspoon black pepper
1 large cabbage, shredded*
4 celery ribs, chopped
1 small green bell pepper, finely chopped
1 (2-ounce) jar diced pimiento, drained

STIR together 1/2 cup sugar and next 5 ingredients in a large bowl; add shredded cabbage, chopped celery, chopped bell pepper, and diced pimiento, and toss to coat. Chill until ready to serve.
*2 (10-ounce) bags angel hair cabbage may be substituted. ▶

below: Easy and doable Stuffed Squash will impress your guests with its fancy-looking presentation.

STUFFED SQUASH

Makes 4 servings
Hands on: 30 min., Hands off: 25 min.

PULP IS SCOOPED FROM COOKED YELLOW SQUASH, LEAVING PERFECTLY INTACT SHELLS FOR STUFFING.

4 yellow squash
1/2 teaspoon salt
2 tablespoons butter or margarine
2 carrots, shredded
1/2 cup chopped green bell pepper
1 small onion, chopped
1/4 teaspoon garlic salt
1/4 teaspoon pepper
1 teaspoon soy sauce

COOK squash and 1/2 teaspoon salt in boiling water to cover in a 2-quart saucepan 10 minutes; drain and cool.
CUT squash in half lengthwise. Scoop out pulp; reserve, leaving 1/4-inch-thick shells.
MELT butter in saucepan over medium heat; add carrots, bell pepper, and onion, and sauté 3 minutes or until crisp-tender. Add garlic salt, pepper, and soy sauce, and cook, stirring often, 5 minutes or until vegetables are tender. Stir in reserved squash pulp. Spoon into squash shells, and place in a 13- x 9-inch pan.
BAKE at 325° for 15 minutes.

POTATO SALAD WITH CUCUMBERS AND TOMATOES

Makes 10 to 12 servings
Hands on: 30 min., Hands off: 30 min.

5 pounds potatoes
2/3 cup olive oil
1/2 cup red wine vinegar
1 1/2 teaspoons salt
1 teaspoon pepper
1/4 cup chopped fresh basil
1 cucumber, peeled, seeded, and
  chopped
2 pints grape or cherry tomatoes
1 large yellow tomato, diced
Garnish: fresh basil sprig

COOK potatoes in boiling salted water to cover 30 minutes or until tender; drain.
COOL potatoes slightly, and cut into 1-inch cubes.
STIR together oil and next 3 ingredients in a large bowl; stir in chopped basil.
ADD potatoes, cucumber, and tomatoes, tossing to coat. Chill until ready to serve. Garnish, if desired.

An olive oil-basil vinaigrette adds a healthy twist to Potato Salad With Cucumbers and Tomatoes.

MANDARIN SALAD

Makes 8 servings
Hands on: 30 min.

1 (3-ounce) package Oriental-flavored
  ramen noodle soup mix
1/2 cup sliced almonds
5 tablespoons sugar, divided
1/2 cup vegetable oil
3 tablespoons white vinegar
1 tablespoon chopped fresh parsley
1/2 teaspoon salt
1/4 teaspoon pepper
1/8 teaspoon hot sauce
1/2 head iceberg lettuce, torn
1/2 head romaine lettuce, torn
5 celery ribs, chopped
2 green onions, chopped
1 (11-ounce) can mandarin orange
  sections, drained

REMOVE flavor packet from soup mix, and set aside. Crumble noodles.
BAKE ramen noodles in a shallow pan at 350° for 10 minutes or until toasted, stirring after 5 minutes. Remove from oven, and cool.
COOK sliced almonds and 3 tablespoons sugar in a small nonstick skillet over medium-low heat, stirring constantly, 5 to 6 minutes or until sugar dissolves and almonds are evenly coated. Remove almonds from heat.

WHISK together reserved flavor packet, oil, next 5 ingredients, and remaining 2 tablespoons sugar in a large bowl. Add lettuces, celery, and onions; toss. Add noodles, almond mixture, and oranges; toss. Serve immediately.

LETTUCE WEDGE SALAD

Makes 4 servings
Hands on: 30 min.

4 to 6 bacon slices
1 medium onion, sliced
1 cup buttermilk
1/2 cup sour cream
1 (1-ounce) envelope Ranch dressing
  mix
1/4 cup chopped fresh basil
2 garlic cloves
1 large head iceberg lettuce, cut into
  4 wedges
Shredded basil (optional)

COOK bacon in a large skillet until crisp; remove bacon, and drain on paper towels, reserving 1 teaspoon drippings in skillet. Crumble bacon, and set aside.
SAUTÉ onion in hot drippings in skillet over medium heat 10 minutes or until tender and lightly browned. Remove from heat; cool.
PROCESS buttermilk and next 4 ingredients in a blender or food processor until

smooth, stopping to scrape down sides. Stir in onion.
TOP each lettuce wedge with dressing; sprinkle with bacon, and, if desired, shredded basil.

FRESH TOMATO DRESSING

Makes 4 cups
Hands on: 20 min., Hands off: 9 hrs.

SERVE THIS DRESSING OVER TOMATO NAPOLEON OR WITH YOUR FAVORITE TOSSED GREENS.

1 cup olive oil
1/2 cup balsamic vinegar
3 garlic cloves, sliced
1 tablespoon sugar
1 tablespoon salt
1 tablespoon pepper
4 large tomatoes, peeled and chopped
2 tablespoons fresh thyme leaves or 4
  thyme sprigs

WHISK together first 6 ingredients in a large glass bowl.
STIR in chopped tomatoes and thyme. Cover and let stand at room temperature 1 hour, stirring occasionally. Cover and chill 8 hours.
NOTE: Dressing may be stored in the refrigerator up to 1 month. Stir additional chopped fresh tomato into dressing after each use.

SNAP BEANS AND POTATOES

Makes 6 servings
Hands on: 30 min., Hands off: 10 min.

4 medium-size red potatoes, peeled
   and quartered (about 1½ pounds)
1 pound fresh green beans, snapped
   into 1½-inch pieces
3 bacon slices
1 large onion, sliced
¼ cup cider vinegar
2 teaspoons dried rosemary, crumbled
¼ teaspoon salt
¼ teaspoon sugar
¼ teaspoon freshly ground pepper

COOK potatoes in boiling salted water to cover in a large saucepan 10 minutes or until tender. Drain and rinse with cold water. Set aside.

COOK beans in boiling salted water to cover in saucepan 3 to 4 minutes or until crisp-tender. Remove from heat; plunge into ice water to stop the cooking process. Drain and set aside.

COOK bacon in a skillet until crisp; remove bacon, reserving drippings in skillet. Crumble bacon, and set aside.

SAUTÉ sliced onion in hot drippings until crisp-tender. Stir in vinegar and next 4 ingredients.

ADD potatoes and beans; cook, stirring occasionally, until thoroughly heated. Toss in bacon.

Cider vinegar and dried rosemary offer a punch of flavor in Snap Beans and Potatoes.

Cut vegetables into thin strips for an eye-catching Herbed Vegetable Medley.

HERBED VEGETABLE MEDLEY

Makes 8 servings
Hands on: 30 min.

3 small zucchini
3 small yellow squash
1 medium-size red bell pepper
2 medium carrots
2 tablespoons butter or vegetable oil
3 garlic cloves, pressed
1 teaspoon salt
1 teaspoon lemon pepper seasoning
⅓ cup chopped green onions
2 tablespoons chopped fresh basil
Garnish: fresh basil sprig

CUT first 4 ingredients into thin strips.

HEAT butter in large skillet over medium-high heat; add garlic, and sauté 1 to 2 minutes. Add carrot strips, salt, and lemon pepper, and sauté 2 to 3 minutes.

ADD remaining vegetable strips, green onions, and chopped basil; sauté 3 minutes or until vegetables are crisp-tender. Garnish, if desired.   ◆

Macaroni and More

Make one of these hearty **recipes** to accompany an entrée, or create a meatless meal by serving your favorite along with a few veggie sides (page 96).

Creamy Four-Cheese Macaroni uses crushed Melba toast for a crisp topping.

HOT GRILLED GRITS

Makes 6 servings
Hands on: 25 min.

1 (10½-ounce) can condensed chicken broth, undiluted
½ cup water
¼ cup butter or margarine
¼ teaspoon salt
1 cup quick-cooking grits, uncooked
1 (8-ounce) loaf pasteurized prepared cheese product, cubed
1 tablespoon pickled jalapeño peppers, minced
1 tablespoon olive oil
Vegetable cooking spray
Salsa (optional)

BRING first 4 ingredients to a boil in a large saucepan over medium heat. Stir in grits; cover, reduce heat, and cook, stirring often, 6 to 8 minutes. Stir in cheese product and peppers until smooth. Pour into a lightly greased 9-inch pieplate; cool until firm.

UNMOLD grits, and cut into 6 wedges; lightly brush each side with oil.

COAT grill rack with cooking spray; place on grill over medium-high heat (350° to 400°). Place wedges on food grate, and grill, covered with lid, 4 minutes on each side or until golden. Serve with salsa, if desired.

CREAMY FOUR-CHEESE MACARONI

Makes 8 servings
Hands on: 15 min., Hands off: 30 min.

SUBSTITUTE YOUR FAVORITE CHEESES FOR ONE OF MORE OF THE SHREDDED VARIETIES WE USE HERE.

2⅔ cups milk
⅓ cup all-purpose flour
¾ cup (3 ounces) shredded fontina or Swiss cheese
½ cup (2 ounces) shredded Parmesan cheese
½ cup (2 ounces) shredded extra-sharp Cheddar cheese
3 ounces light processed cheese spread
3 cups elbow macaroni, cooked
½ teaspoon pepper
⅓ cup crushed onion Melba toast (about 12 pieces)
1 tablespoon butter or margarine, softened

WHISK together milk and flour in a large saucepan; cook over medium heat, whisking constantly, 8 minutes or until thickened. Add cheeses, and cook, whisking often, 3 minutes or until cheeses melt. Stir in macaroni and pepper. Spoon into a lightly greased 2-quart baking dish.

COMBINE crushed Melba toast and butter in a small bowl; stir until well blended. Sprinkle over macaroni mixture.

BAKE at 375° for 30 minutes or until cheese is bubbly.

ROASTED NEW POTATOES WITH ROSEMARY AND GARLIC

Makes 4 servings
Hands on: 10 min., Hands off: 30 min.

2 pounds small red potatoes, cut into
    1-inch cubes
3 tablespoons olive oil
1 teaspoon minced garlic
2 teaspoons chopped fresh or dried
    rosemary
3/4 teaspoon salt
1/2 teaspoon pepper

TOSS together all ingredients in a large bowl. Spoon into a lightly greased 15- x 10-inch jelly-roll pan.
BAKE at 450° for 25 to 30 minutes or until potatoes are tender.

LEMON-HERB RICE

Makes 4 servings
Hands on: 15 min., Hands off: 17 min.

1 cup uncooked long-grain rice
1 tablespoon olive oil
1 small onion, chopped
1 tablespoon minced garlic
1 (14-ounce) can chicken broth
1 1/2 tablespoons fresh lemon juice
3 green onions, sliced
2 teaspoons chopped fresh basil
1 teaspoon grated lemon rind
1/2 teaspoon salt
1/4 teaspoon pepper

SAUTÉ rice in hot oil in a large saucepan over medium heat 2 minutes. Add onion and garlic; sauté 3 minutes. Stir in broth and lemon juice; bring to a boil. Cover, reduce heat, and simmer 10 to 12 minutes or until rice is tender. Remove from heat; stir in green onions and remaining ingredients. Cover and let stand 5 minutes.

LEMON COUSCOUS

Makes 4 to 6 servings
Hands on: 10 min., Hands off: 10 min.

2 (5.4-ounce) packages toasted pine
    nut couscous mix
2 cups fat-free reduced-sodium
    chicken broth
1 tablespoon grated lemon rind
1/3 cup fresh lemon juice
2 teaspoons butter or margarine
2 tablespoons chopped fresh parsley
1/3 cup diced red bell pepper

REMOVE seasoning packets from couscous packages.
COMBINE broth, next 3 ingredients, and seasoning packets in a medium saucepan; bring to a boil over medium-high heat. Stir in couscous; cover, remove from heat, and let stand 10 minutes. Stir in parsley and red bell pepper. Serve immediately.
NOTE: For testing purposes only, we used Near East Toasted Pine Nut Couscous Mix.

BLUE CHEESE POTATOES

Makes 3 to 4 servings
Hands on: 20 min., Hands off: 1 hr.

TO KEEP NEW POTATO SHELLS FROM BREAKING APART, USE A SMALL MELON BALLER TO SCOOP OUT PULP.

6 to 8 new potatoes (about 1/2 pound)
2 tablespoons butter or margarine
1 cup fresh baby spinach
1/4 cup chopped onion
1/2 cup crumbled blue cheese
2 tablespoons softened cream cheese
1 teaspoon lemon juice

BAKE potatoes at 400° for 45 minutes or until tender; cool.
CUT potatoes in half lengthwise. Carefully scoop out pulp, leaving 1/4-inch-thick shells. Beat pulp at medium speed with an electric mixer until smooth.
MELT butter in a skillet over medium heat; add spinach and onion, and sauté until spinach wilts. Remove from heat. Stir in potato pulp, cheeses, and lemon juice. Spoon into shells, and place on a baking sheet.
BAKE at 400° for 15 minutes or until thoroughly heated.

MICROWAVE RISOTTO

Makes 6 to 8 servings
Hands on: 30 min., Hands off: 5 min.

1 tablespoon butter or margarine
1 tablespoon olive oil
1 cup uncooked Arborio rice
1/2 cup chopped onion
3 cups chicken broth
1 (8-ounce) package sliced fresh
    mushrooms
1 cup frozen sweet peas
1 cup freshly grated Parmesan cheese
1/4 teaspoon freshly ground pepper

MICROWAVE butter and oil at HIGH 2 minutes in a large microwave-safe bowl; stir in rice and onion. Microwave at HIGH 4 minutes, stirring after 3 minutes.
STIR in broth; microwave at HIGH 10 minutes, stirring at 3-minute intervals.
STIR in mushrooms, and microwave at HIGH 8 minutes, stirring at 3-minute intervals.
STIR in peas; microwave at HIGH 2 minutes. Cover and let stand 5 minutes.
SPRINKLE with cheese and pepper; serve immediately.   ◆

For something out of the ordinary, serve Veggie Pancakes with sour cream and salsa.

VEGGIE PANCAKES

Makes 10 servings
Hands on: 25 min.

1 (6-ounce) package self-rising
    white cornmeal mix
1 (11-ounce) can whole kernel corn,
    drained
1/2 large red bell pepper, chopped
7 green onions, thinly sliced
1 large carrot, shredded
2/3 cup buttermilk
1 large egg, lightly beaten
1/2 cup all-purpose flour
1/2 teaspoon dried crushed red
    pepper
1/4 cup vegetable oil, divided
Toppings: sour cream, salsa
Garnishes: chopped fresh cilantro,
    leaf lettuce

STIR together first 9 ingredients.
HEAT 2 tablespoons oil in a large nonstick skillet. Drop half of batter by 1/3 cupfuls into hot oil, and cook 3 to 4 minutes on each side or until golden. Keep warm.
REPEAT procedure with remaining oil and batter. Serve pancakes with desired toppings. Garnish, if desired.

Easy Baked Breads

Slather honey and butter on toasted slices of Peanut Butter Bread.

Yes, these recipes really are ready for the oven in 20 minutes or less. Just stir the batter or prepare the refrigerated dough, and you are well on your way to the perfect accompaniment to any meal.

PEANUT BUTTER BREAD

Makes 1 (9-inch) loaf
Hands on: 15 min., Hands off: 1 hr.

2 cups all-purpose flour
½ cup sugar
2 teaspoons baking powder
1 teaspoon salt
¾ cup creamy or crunchy peanut butter
1 large egg
1 cup milk

STIR together first 4 ingredients in a medium bowl.
CUT in peanut butter with a fork or pastry blender until crumbly.
STIR together egg and milk; stir into dry ingredients just until moistened. Pour batter into a greased 9- x 5-inch loafpan.
BAKE at 350° for 1 hour or until a wooden pick inserted in center comes out clean. Remove from pan immediately, and cool on a wire rack.
PEANUT BUTTER MUFFINS: Spoon batter into greased muffin pans, filling two-thirds full. Stir together ½ cup uncooked regular oats; 2 tablespoons golden raisins, chopped; 2 tablespoons honey; and 1 tablespoon butter or margarine, melted. Spoon oats mixture evenly over batter. Bake at 350° for 25 to 30 minutes. Makes 1 dozen. Hands on: 20 min., Hands off: 30 min.

BROCCOLI CORNBREAD MUFFINS

Makes 2 dozen mini muffins
Hands on: 20 min., Hands off: 23 min.

1 (8½-ounce) package corn muffin mix
1 (10-ounce) package frozen chopped broccoli, thawed
1 cup (4 ounces) shredded Cheddar cheese
1 small onion, chopped
2 large eggs
½ cup butter or margarine, melted and slightly cooled

COMBINE first 4 ingredients in a large bowl; make a well in center of mixture.
STIR together eggs and butter, blending well; add to broccoli mixture, stirring just until dry ingredients are moistened.
SPOON into lightly greased mini muffin pans, filling three-fourths full.
BAKE at 325° for 15 to 20 minutes or until golden. Let stand 2 to 3 minutes before removing from pans.

HAM-AND-CHEDDAR MUFFINS

Makes 12 muffins
Hands on: 20 min., Hands off: 21 min.

3 tablespoons butter or margarine
1 medium-size sweet onion, finely
    chopped
1½ cups all-purpose baking mix
2 cups (8 ounces) shredded Cheddar
    cheese, divided
½ cup milk
1 large egg
1 cup finely chopped cooked ham
Poppy seeds (optional)

MELT butter in a skillet over medium-high heat; add onion, and sauté 3 to 5 minutes or until tender. Set aside.

COMBINE 1½ cups baking mix and 1 cup cheese in a large bowl; make a well in center of mixture.

STIR together ½ cup milk and 1 egg, blending well; add to cheese mixture, stirring just until dry ingredients are moistened. Stir in sautéed onion and 1 cup chopped ham.

SPOON into lightly greased muffin pans, filling two-thirds full. Sprinkle evenly with remaining 1 cup cheese. Sprinkle with poppy seeds, if desired.

BAKE at 425° for 18 minutes or until golden. Let stand 2 to 3 minutes before removing from pans.

NOTE: Substitute mini muffin pans for regular pans, if desired. Bake at 425° for 14 minutes or until golden. Makes 2½ dozen mini muffins. For testing purposes only, we used Bisquick All-Purpose Baking Mix.

REDUCED-FAT HAM-AND-CHEDDAR MUFFINS: Substitute low-fat baking mix, fat-free or low-fat shredded Cheddar cheese, and fat-free milk. Reduce butter to 1 tablespoon. Proceed as directed.

HAM-AND-SWISS MUFFINS: Substitute shredded Swiss cheese for Cheddar; whisk in 2 tablespoons Dijon mustard with milk and egg. Proceed as directed.

SAUSAGE-AND-CHEESE MUFFINS: Substitute 1 cup hot or mild ground pork sausage, cooked and crumbled, for chopped ham. Proceed as directed.

CHICKEN-AND-GREEN CHILE MUFFINS: Substitute 1 cup finely chopped cooked chicken for ham and 2 cups shredded Mexican four-cheese blend for Cheddar; add 1 (4.5-ounce) can chopped green chiles to batter. Proceed as directed.

SESAME-CHEESE MUFFINS

Makes 8 muffins
Hands on: 20 min., Hands off: 20 min.

1 tablespoon butter
1 small sweet onion, finely chopped
1½ cups all-purpose baking mix
1 cup (4 ounces) shredded sharp
    Cheddar cheese, divided*
1 large egg
½ cup milk
1 teaspoon sesame seeds, toasted
2 tablespoons butter, melted

MELT 1 tablespoon butter in a small skillet over medium-high heat. Add onion, and sauté 2 minutes or until tender; set aside.

COMBINE baking mix and ½ cup cheese in large bowl; make well in center of mixture.

STIR together onion, egg, and milk, blending well; add to cheese mixture, stirring just until dry ingredients are moistened.

SPOON into lightly greased muffin pans, filling two-thirds full. Sprinkle evenly with remaining ½ cup cheese and sesame seeds; drizzle with melted butter.

BAKE at 400° for 15 to 20 minutes or until muffins are golden.

*1 cup shredded Monterey Jack cheese with peppers may be substituted.

NOTE: Substitute mini muffin pans for regular pans, if desired. Bake at 400° for 12 to 14 minutes or until golden. Makes 1½ dozen mini muffins. For testing purposes only, we used Bisquick All-Purpose Baking Mix.   ◆

SOUTHWESTERN KNOTS

Makes 12 servings
Hands on: 15 min., Hands off: 15 min.

2½ tablespoons butter or margarine,
    melted
¼ teaspoon chili powder
¼ teaspoon ground cumin
1 (11-ounce) can refrigerated
    breadsticks

STIR together first 3 ingredients until blended.

UNROLL breadsticks. Separate each dough portion; loosely tie each portion into a knot, and place, 1 inch apart, on an ungreased baking sheet. Brush evenly with butter mixture.

Just three ingredients—butter, chili powder, and cumin—are brushed onto refrigerated breadsticks to make Southwestern Knots. **right:** To get this look, simply tie each dough strip as you would a knot.

BAKE at 350° for 15 minutes or until breadsticks are golden.

ITALIAN BREAD KNOTS: Substitute ¼ teaspoon Italian seasoning for chili powder and cumin. Sprinkle bread knots with 1 tablespoon grated Parmesan cheese. Proceed as directed.

CAJUN BREAD KNOTS: Substitute ½ teaspoon Cajun seasoning for chili powder and cumin. Add ¼ teaspoon dried thyme, if desired. Proceed as directed.

The **refreshing flavors** of nature's bounty are perfect for after dinner. All these desserts feature fresh fruits or berries, and some can be prepared in advance—just follow the make-ahead tips included with the recipes.

LEMON-RASPBERRY PARFAITS

Makes 4 to 6 servings
Hands on: 30 min.

PREPARE THE PUDDING AND WHIPPED CREAM LAYERS AHEAD, AND CHILL UP TO 8 HOURS, IF DESIRED.

1 cup granulated sugar
¼ cup all-purpose flour
1 cup half-and-half
½ cup lemon juice
2 egg yolks
¼ cup butter or margarine
½ cup sour cream
2 tablespoons seedless raspberry preserves
½ cup powdered sugar
1 cup whipping cream
1 pint fresh raspberries

COOK first 5 ingredients in a 3-quart saucepan over medium heat, whisking constantly, 10 minutes or until thickened. Remove pudding from heat, and whisk in ¼ cup butter. Cool and chill until ready to assemble.

STIR together sour cream, preserves, and powdered sugar.

BEAT whipping cream at medium speed with an electric mixer until stiff peaks form. Fold in sour cream mixture; chill.

SPOON half of pudding, raspberries, and whipped cream mixture evenly into 4 to 6 parfait glasses. Top evenly with remaining pudding; sprinkle with remaining raspberries. Top evenly with remaining whipped cream mixture.

Fruit Finishes

Port wine adds a grown-up twist to Watermelon Sorbet. Substitute white grape juice for a kid-friendly version.

WATERMELON SORBET

Makes 2 quarts
Hands on: 20 min., Hands off: 1 hr. plus freeze time

1½ cups sugar
1½ cups water
6 cups peeled, seeded, and cubed watermelon
½ cup tawny port wine or white grape juice
¼ cup lemon juice

BRING 1½ cups sugar and 1½ cups water to a boil over medium-high heat, stirring occasionally until sugar dissolves. Reduce heat, and simmer 5 minutes. Remove from heat, and cool.

PROCESS watermelon in a food processor until smooth. Pour watermelon puree through a fine wire-mesh strainer into a bowl, discarding pulp.

COMBINE sugar syrup, watermelon puree, wine, and lemon juice in freezer container of 1-gallon electric freezer; freeze according to manufacturer's instructions. (Instructions and times will vary.) Let stand 1 hour before serving.

Strawberry Trifle is an eye-pleasing addition to an outdoor menu.

VERY BERRY COBBLER

Makes 6 servings
Hands on: 20 min., Hands off: 45 min.

½ cup butter or margarine
1½ cups fresh or frozen blueberries, thawed
1½ cups fresh strawberries, halved
2 tablespoons sugar
½ teaspoon grated lemon rind
¼ to ½ teaspoon ground cardamom (optional)
1 cup sugar
½ cup chopped walnuts or pecans, toasted
1¼ cups all-purpose flour
2 teaspoons baking powder
1 cup milk
Vanilla ice cream

MELT butter in a shallow 8-inch square baking dish in a 350° oven. Set aside.
TOSS together blueberries, next 3 ingredients, and, if desired, cardamom.
COMBINE 1 cup sugar and next 3 ingredients. Stir in milk until blended. Pour into baking dish; spoon berry mixture into center of batter. (Do not stir.)
BAKE at 350° for 40 to 45 minutes. Serve warm with vanilla ice cream. ◆

STRAWBERRY TRIFLE

Makes 14 servings
Hands on: 45 min.

MAKE THE CUSTARD THE NIGHT BEFORE FOR EASY ASSEMBLY.

5 cups sliced fresh strawberries
2 (10-ounce) angel food cakes, cut into 1-inch cubes
6 tablespoons strawberry liqueur*
Custard
½ cup strawberry preserves
2 cups whipping cream
¼ cup powdered sugar
Garnishes: whole strawberry, toasted sliced almonds

ARRANGE ½ cup strawberry slices along lower edge of a 14-cup trifle bowl. Place half of cake cubes in bowl. Drizzle with 2 tablespoons liqueur. Top cake cubes with 2 cups strawberries; drizzle with 2 tablespoons liqueur. Spoon 2 cups Custard over strawberries. Arrange ½ cup strawberries along edge of bowl. Top with remaining cake cubes. Drizzle with remaining 2 tablespoons liqueur. Spoon remaining 2 cups strawberries over cake cubes. Spread preserves over strawberries; spoon remaining 2 cups Custard over preserves.
BEAT whipping cream until foamy; gradually add powdered sugar, beating until soft peaks form. Spread over trifle.

Garnish, if desired. Serve immediately.
*Strawberry syrup may be substituted.

Custard:
Makes 4 cups
Hands on: 25 min.

1¾ cups milk
⅓ cup cornstarch
2 cups half-and-half
4 egg yolks
¾ cup sugar
2 teaspoons vanilla extract

COOK ½ cup milk and cornstarch in a large saucepan over medium heat, stirring well. Add half-and half and remaining 1¼ cups milk; cook, stirring constantly, until thickened.
BEAT egg yolks and ¾ cup sugar at medium speed with an electric mixer until thick and pale. Gradually stir about one-fourth of hot mixture into egg mixture; add to remaining hot mixture, stirring constantly. Cook over low heat, stirring constantly, 1 to 2 minutes or until thickened. Remove from heat; stir in 2 teaspoons vanilla extract, and cool. Cover and chill custard until ready to serve.

Light and Luscious

For a conveniently portable dessert or a delicious gift, make these tasty Lemon Squares.

Just because you're watching your calories doesn't mean you have to give up desserts. Our deliciously lightened favorites—from pound cake to cobbler—are just as heavenly as their traditional versions, but these won't leave you with a guilty conscience.

CARAMEL CUSTARD

Makes 6 servings
Hands on: 30 min.; Hands off: 4 hrs., 30 min.
EGG WHITES AND LOW-FAT MILK LIGHTEN THIS SMOOTH, RICH CUSTARD.

1¼ cups sugar, divided
½ teaspoon fresh lemon juice
2½ cups low-fat milk
6 egg whites
2 large eggs
1 tablespoon vanilla extract

SPRINKLE ½ cup sugar in a small heavy saucepan; place over medium-high heat. Add lemon juice, and cook, shaking pan constantly, 2 to 3 minutes or until sugar melts and turns a light golden brown. Quickly pour hot sugar mixture into 6 (4-ounce) baking dishes, tilting each to coat bottoms evenly. (Mixture may crack slightly as it cools.)
COOK 2½ cups milk and ¼ cup sugar in a small heavy saucepan over medium-high heat, stirring constantly, 6 minutes or until hot and frothy. (Do not boil.) Remove from heat.
SPRINKLE remaining ½ cup sugar in a large heavy saucepan; place over medium-high heat. Cook, shaking constantly, 2 to 3 minutes or until sugar melts and turns a light golden brown; remove from heat. Gradually add hot milk mixture, whisking constantly.

LEMON SQUARES

Makes 2 dozen
Hands on: 20 min., Hands off: 40 min.

1 cup all-purpose flour
⅓ cup powdered sugar
⅓ cup butter or margarine, cut into small pieces
1 cup granulated sugar
2 tablespoons all-purpose flour
½ teaspoon baking powder
¼ teaspoon salt
3 egg whites
1 large egg
½ cup frozen lemon juice, thawed*
1½ teaspoons grated lemon rind
¼ teaspoon butter extract
2 tablespoons powdered sugar

COMBINE 1 cup flour and ⅓ cup powdered sugar; cut in butter with a pastry blender until crumbly. Press firmly into bottom of a lightly greased 11- x 7-inch baking dish.
BAKE at 350° for 20 minutes or until lightly browned.
WHISK together granulated sugar and next 8 ingredients until blended; pour over crust.
BAKE at 350° for 20 minutes or until set. Cool on a wire rack. Cut into squares, and sprinkle evenly with 2 tablespoons powdered sugar.
*½ cup fresh lemon juice may be substituted for frozen lemon juice.
NOTE: For testing purposes only, we used Minute Maid Premium 100% Pure Lemon Juice From Concentrate found in the freezer section.

WHISK together egg whites and eggs in a large bowl; gradually add hot milk mixture, whisking constantly. Stir in vanilla. Pour custard evenly over caramelized sugar in baking dishes. Place baking dishes in a shallow roasting pan; add hot water to pan to a depth of 1 inch.

BAKE at 300° for 1 hour and 30 minutes or until a knife inserted in center comes out clean. Remove baking dishes from water; cool on a wire rack. Cover and chill at least 3 hours.

RUN a knife around edge of custards to loosen; invert onto serving plates. Drizzle custards with any syrup remaining in baking dishes.

FRENCH TOAST-PEACH COBBLER

Makes 10 servings
Hands on: 30 min., Hands off: 1 hr.

THE NATURAL SWEETNESS OF ORANGE JUICE AND ZEST ADDS A CITRUS TWIST TO THE FRENCH TOAST COATING, WHICH IS LIGHTENED WITH REDUCED-FAT MARGARINE AND EGG WHITES.

12 large peaches, peeled and sliced*
1 cup sugar, divided
2 tablespoons all-purpose flour
1 teaspoon grated orange rind
⅓ cup fresh orange juice
¼ cup light margarine, melted
¼ teaspoon ground cinnamon
3 egg whites
8 (1.5-ounce) slices hearty white bread
2 tablespoons sugar

STIR together peaches, ¾ cup sugar, and 2 tablespoons flour in a lightly greased 13- x 9-inch baking dish; let stand 30 minutes, stirring occasionally.

WHISK together orange rind, next 4 ingredients, and remaining ¼ cup sugar in a shallow bowl; set aside.

TRIM crusts from bread slices, and cut each slice into 2 triangles.

DIP each triangle of bread into egg mixture, and arrange evenly over peach mixture. Sprinkle with 2 tablespoons sugar.

BAKE at 350° for 45 minutes or until cobbler is golden.

*3 (16-ounce) bags frozen sliced peaches, thawed, may be substituted for 12 large peaches.

NOTE: For testing purposes only, we used Pepperidge Farm Farmhouse Hearty White bread. ◆

BLUEBERRY POUND CAKE

Makes 16 servings
Hands on: 20 min.; Hands off: 1 hr., 25 min.

OUR FRIENDS AT Cooking Light MAGAZINE ORIGINALLY DEVELOPED THIS DESSERT. WE THINK IT TASTES JUST AS RICH AS A FULL-FAT POUND CAKE.

2 cups granulated sugar
½ cup light butter
½ (8-ounce) package ⅓-less-fat cream cheese, softened
3 large eggs
1 egg white
3 cups all-purpose flour
2 cups fresh or frozen blueberries, thawed
1 teaspoon baking powder
½ teaspoon baking soda
½ teaspoon salt
1 (8-ounce) container low-fat lemon yogurt
2 teaspoons vanilla extract
½ cup powdered sugar
4 teaspoons lemon juice

BEAT first 3 ingredients at medium speed with an electric mixer until blended. Add eggs and egg white, 1 at a time, beating until blended after each addition.

TOSS together 2 tablespoons flour and 2 cups blueberries in a small bowl. Combine baking powder, baking soda, salt, and remaining flour; add to sugar mixture alternately with yogurt, beginning and ending with flour mixture. Beat at low speed just until blended after each addition. Fold in blueberry mixture and vanilla; pour batter into a lightly greased 10-inch tube pan.

BAKE at 350° for 1 hour and 15 minutes. Cool in pan on a wire rack 10 minutes. Remove from pan.

STIR together powdered sugar and lemon juice in a small bowl; drizzle over warm cake. Cut with a serrated knife.

A simple powdered sugar-and-lemon juice glaze dresses up Blueberry Pound Cake.

Six Easy Menus

Looking for something new and delicious to put on the table? Choose any of these sensational combinations for casual get-togethers or weeknight meals. Or flip through the pages of this book for even more tasty options.

Weekend Brunch
Page 88
Brie-and-Sausage Brunch Casserole
Spiced Apples
Pecan Crescent Twists
Mulled Cranberry Drink

Casual Dinner Party
Page 92
Pork Medallions in Mustard Sauce
Carrot-Sweet Potato Puree
Green Beans With Caramelized Onions
Sour Cream Yeast Rolls
Grown-up Hot Chocolate
Pecan Toffee

Spring Picnic
Page 80
Smoked Turkey Wraps
Fresh Pesto Pasta Salad
potato chips
bottled soft drinks

Chicken Tonight
Page 16
Benne Seed Chicken
Lettuce Wedge Salad
Herbed Vegetable Medley
cornbread
sweet tea

Southern Catfish Fry
Page 62
Fried Catfish
baked beans
Creamy Sweet Slaw
Buttermilk Hush Puppies
bottled soft drinks or sweet tea

Garden Gathering
Page 84
Lemon Flank Steak Skewers
Chilled Shrimp With Rémoulade Sauce
Balsamic Marinated Olives
crusty bread
Spicy Jack Cheese Crisps
Mint Bellinis
Creamy Citrus Tartlets

recipe **index**